HITLER'S FALL GUYS

HITLER'S FALL GUYS

An Examination of the Luftwaffe
by One of America's Most Famous Aces

Col. Walker "Bud" Mahurin

USAF (Ret.)

Schiffer Military History
Atglen, PA

Acknowledgements
I wish to thank Valerie Miller, my stepdaughter, for her great assistance in helping me convert a typewritten manuscript to the computer format. Without her help I would still be trying to understand my computer. My daughter, Lynn, and her husband Larry Vaughan have been kind enough to provide office space for me and have given me support in writing. Col. Ray Toliver and Trevor Constable have been a great help in answering questions related to the *Luftwaffe* and members of the German Fighter Pilot's Association.

Finally, Dick Freeman has been of great help in finding mistakes in the manuscript. His knowledge of the aerial activity during WWII gave credence to his support of this effort while it was being written.

Book Design by Robert Biondi.

Printed in China
ISBN: 0-7643-0871-8

We are interested in hearing from authors with book ideas on military topics.

Published by Schiffer Publishing Ltd.
4880 Lower Valley Road
Atglen, PA 19310 USA
Phone: (610) 593-1777
FAX: (610) 593-2002
E-mail: Schifferbk@aol.com.
Visit our web site at: www.schifferbooks.com
Please write for a free catalog.
This book may be purchased from the publisher.
Please include $3.95 postage.
Try your bookstore first.

In Europe, Schiffer books are distributed by:
Bushwood Books
6 Marksbury Road
Kew Gardens
Surrey TW9 4JF
England
Phone: 44 (0)181 392-8585
FAX: 44 (0)181 392-9876
E-mail: Bushwd@aol.com.

Try your bookstore first.

Contents

Preface

Shortly after WWII ended some twelve high ranking *Luftwaffe* officers were taken to England to be interrogated as to their activities during
the war. These interrogations took place at Kaufbueren, Germany and the
Latimer House in England from 20 September to 4 October 1945. The
reports of these interrogations were very extensive and constituted a bible
of how the German *Luftwaffe* conducted its battle for the skies over most
of Europe. Obviously, the airmen involved were the most experienced in
all phases of the aerial battle and represented top level commanders and
their views. The reports thus generated, involved lessons learned as well
as critical comments made of the political leaders of the time and information that was of great value to the Air Forces of then Allies during the
years of the cold war.

Eventually, this documentation that included actual copies of orders
and regulations issued about *Luftwaffe* High Command proved to be of
value when considered by the Air Fore in Europe when it came time to re-
establish a new *Luftwaffe* that could be aligned with the rest of the NATO
nations air forces. Efforts had been made to find individuals (both officers and airmen) with *Luftwaffe* experience who would be the foundation
of the new *Luftwaffe*. This effort was well under way shortly after the war
ended. Much of this action was taken as a result of the attitude of the
Russian Government, which seemed to be aimed at negating peaceful

solutions to rebuilding not only Germany, but also the rest of war torn Europe.

In the later part of the 1950s, a group of individuals who were either retired or active duty Air Force officers decided to form the American Fighter Aces Association. Having heard of a like organization called "The German Fighter Pilot's Association" it seemed that there was a need in the United States in order to keep our youth interested in becoming fighter pilots, considering this to be an extremely honorable military profession. With this new organization holding annual conventions, information was presented regarding the activities of the German Association and it had been learned that the GFPA had created a monument and through the efforts of Colonel Ray Toliver, the AFPA received an invitation to attend a dedication ceremony in Germany at the new memorial.

Six members of the AFAA, (myself included) were flown by military air to Germany to attend the function and were met by representatives of the GFPA upon landing. Escorted by members of the GFPA, the Air Force representatives were privileged to make a contribution to the memorial as well as to make a short address commemorating the heroism of the pilots who had fallen to their deaths throughout the world.

Following was a week long program sponsored by the *Luftwaffe* and the members of the GFPA allowing the American guests to visit three different annual reunions attended by GFPA members. The reason for the three reunions was to allow members who were not affluent to attend a reunion in their local region without having to defray the cost of traveling great distances to be there. This was a great boon to some of the less fortunate members and since arrangements were made for us, it was a great help to us also. Many German Aces were able to attend all three locations and this was helpful to us in getting to know many of them. As it was, we had an opportunity to discuss the aerial war during WWII frankly and honestly although we had all been enemies at one time or another during the war.

By this time, many of the higher ranking officers in the old *Luftwaffe* had now become officials in the new organization and during one of our visits we were able to discuss the conduct of the war from the senior leadership standpoint as well as the standpoint of the pilots who had been engaged in actual combat. Obviously, General Adolf Galland was a leader in many of these discussions, although there were a number of other officers who were classified as "*experten*" willing to compare notes with us as we met in a social environment. These discussions were most revealing and focused mainly on where the *Luftwaffe* leadership had failed Germany and had additionally failed the fighter forces. Since so many pilots had been killed during the war as a result of these failures, it struck us as visitors that this story could easily repeat itself unless nations of the free world were vigilant.

Some time after this visit, Colonel Hub Zemke who had been commander of the 56th Fighter Group in England during the war, sent me a copy of the intelligence reports of the interrogations of senior *Luftwaffe* officials at the end of the war in both German and English. This was a weighty document that included a great amount of detail of how the *Luftwaffe* carried out its missions as well as why they eventually failed in defending Germany. It was apparent that the Germans were rigid in constructing regulations for their pilots as to how to carry out all phases of aerial combat almost down to the last detail. The document also included straight forward comments about the failure of the higher command to grasp opportunities for success and how failures almost always came about because the high command answered to a dictator who was greatly feared by those closest to him.

For many years it seemed to be of little value to exploit this document because the world was rapidly changing. However, as time had gone by, our nation has faced several crises in various conflicts and often this has resulted in disasters because these were directed by those with no training or experience. This has been especially true because there has been limited understanding as to the impact of morale as related to victory and statistics alone are not a true indication of how military organization can function victoriously.

The purpose of this manuscript is to point out what can happen if the weapons of war are misdirected, not only to harm the people involved, but also to harm our nation as a whole. Members of the military services can get killed, families can suffer, and the expense of war is staggering yet diplomacy can fail and a nation can declare war. Eventually, people must sit down at a table to discuss peace and unfortunately, there is always a great effort made to lay the blame on others. This nation is the most powerful in the world, but who helped make it so? Perhaps all of us had a share in this success. Still the opportunities we have around us are too valuable to misuse.

We got to know our enemies only to find them to be friends. Survivors of the war in Europe were forced by their leaders to suffer great difficulties at the end of the war, not because they didn't do their best, but because the leaders were too involved in striving for advancement, for political favors or for petty jealous reasons. They thought only of themselves and thus brought their nation to its knees. Everyone lost. The people we have met over the years exemplify all of the values we hope our children will have when it comes their time to carry on the torch of freedom. I hope this effort will bring out an understanding of what those values mean because we only go this way once, and unfortunately, we can't come back and do it all over again to get it right.

Introduction

So many books have been written over the years about the air war in Germany during WW II that it seems impossible that any detail would be missing. Yet, increasing interest in the events that transpired then has resulted in more and more distorted information on the subject until those battles almost seem to be bright, clean and courageous engagements between the best of pilots instead of the terrible death laden missions they really were. Major events tend to become distorted over the years anyway, and often, individual points of view change as additional facts come to light with time. What follows is a different perspective of those battles and the events that led up to them. Told by outstanding leaders of the *Luftwaffe* at a time when they were being interrogated by Allied Intelligence at Kaufbeuren, Germany in the summer of 1945 while the events of the war were fresh in mind.

There has been no effort to change the direct and accurate story related by these airmen. However, this documentation has been augmented by views of the author in light of changes and circumstances that were taking place in the Allied Air Forces at the time. Additionally, personal experiences coupled with volumes of written information have been used to present a comparison of the adversaries.

Since this story goes back to the early days of the *Luftwaffe* shortly after World War I, it has been told in a historic light. Starting with the

Spanish Civil War, these high-ranking officers who were fighter pilots discussed the *Luftwaffe*, how it started, how it grew, where it was going, and what went wrong.

These were the viewpoints of men who believed in the new *Reich*. They were young men who could not possibly understand the pitfalls of aggression, the intricacies of diplomacy or the impact of world power politics at the time. Their motivation was closer in the responsibility of command, the adulation accorded a hero, the thrill of victory, and the fast clean life in the air that led to a high sense of achievement ... initially! Later, the motivation became simple. Defend the homeland and loved ones living there and try to survive.

Although they realized that defeat was inevitable these men struggled against overwhelming odds to turn back the attacking air armadas. Time after time they and their fellow pilots took to the air only to parachute, crash, be wounded or killed in a futile effort to stop the maelstrom brought on their country by a mad leader who refused to recognize reality. Accurate figures are not available regarding the total number of pilots trained in the *Luftwaffe* from the time of the Spanish Civil War until the end. However, the German Fighter Pilot's Association of today has less than one thousand members who survived the war in the air. Most of the surviving fighter pilots suffered a double tragedy. Not only did they lose friends, relatives, and loved ones during the war but Hitler and Göring blamed them for the defeat of Germany. Rather than accepting the blame for astounding and disastrous decisions these two men made time and again, they tried to shift responsibility to the fighter pilot in the cockpit because he was to be the "Fall Guy."

Perhaps the most well known and certainly the most outstanding survivor was General Adolf Galland, who authored a book after the war entitled, *The First And The Last*. His remarks during interrogation in the early part of 1945 are a major part of this chronicle.

In a foreword of a book written about the *Luftwaffe* by John Killan, Sir John Slessor, Marshal of the Royal Air Force, quoted Field Marshal Smuts as follows: "You know, it's a great mistake to imagine that it is great victories that win wars. On the contrary, it is the great blunders. We ought to put up a statue in Trafalgar Square to Hitler for having been such a fool as to attack Russia."

CHAPTER ONE

In the Beginning

In February 1936, the French Chamber of Deputies approved a Franco-Soviet Pact, 353 votes to 164, and Hitler used this act as a pretext to re-occupy the demilitarized zone of the Rhineland, Aachen, Trier, and Saarbrucken. The *Luftwaffe*, with little more than a collection of old and new aircraft was completely unequipped even for this small military operation, and the only flying school in existence then training fighter pilots had to be disbanded because the aircraft were needed elsewhere. Whatever aircraft were available throughout Germany were flown to various airfields to be viewed by the press and the public, each time being painted with a different color scheme to give the impression of large numbers. Pilots, too, were in short supply, so mechanics were dressed in pilot's uniforms and photographed beside aircraft they couldn't fly. But the scheme worked so well that the whole world accepted this sham as evidence of the emergence of new air power for Germany.

Prior to these events, Mussolini had been conducting a war, modern for the period, against Emperor Haile Selassie's tribesmen in Ethiopia, and most of the major powers in Europe were preoccupied with futile attempts to bring this unwarranted aggression to a halt. Aided by this unrest, Hitler consolidated his gains in the Rhineland by dissolving the Reichstag and holding a re-election, which he won, by a popular vote of 99% of the German electorate. In July 1936, a civil war broke out in

Spain, greatly adding to the confusion already existent in South West Europe.

This last unhappy event was seized upon as an excellent opportunity to become a proving ground for testing military equipment and tactics under operational conditions by several great and powerful nations of Europe who expected valuable experience would be gained. Russia sent quantities of I-15 and I-16 fighters and SB-2 bombers to the Communist Government Forces in Spain, as did the French. Both Mussolini and Hitler decided to provide both men and equipment to General Francisco Franco, the leader of the revolutionary forces, and thousands of men together with hundreds of tons of equipment were sent into Spain in the following three years. If the Spanish had been left to fight out their own problems, possibly much bloodshed would have been avoided in view of the fact that both sides were evenly matched in the beginning, especially in the air. But this was not to be, since both sides began to receive assistance from foreign countries. The *Luftwaffe* contribution to this arena was a "Volunteer" Corps officially known by the numerical designation of "188", but popularly known as the Legion Kondor. Among members of this elite group of men was Adolf Galland, a man who was destined to become the leader of the German Fighter Force.

Luftwaffe personnel, who were chosen for service in Spain, were equipped with civilian clothes, various items of identification and Spanish money given to them by a secret office in Berlin which was set up to conceal the identity of the entire operation. Most of those selected were enthusiastic about this assignment because it meant an appointment to a rank one grade higher than their normal status with a corresponding increase in pay. It developed that this was more than earned by most of them in the long run. The next stage of the journey into Spain came when groups of "volunteers" were transferred to Doberitz a central assembly point. Dressed in civilian clothes and pretending to be "Kraft Durch Freude" (Strength through Joy) tourists, all sorts of maintenance and support personnel moved to Hamburg for embarkation, supposedly bound for Genoa, Italy, but, in reality, headed for Spain.

Problems of contact between loved ones and the "tourists" were solved by establishing a mail drop, c/o Max Winkler, Berlin, SW 6811. Anyone wishing to correspond with members of the Kondor Legion forwarded through this agency. The first groups departed Hamburg on the SS Usaramo along with a number of He 51 fighters and spare parts for the Ju 52 bombers that had already flown to Spanish bases under the guidance of Hisma Air Transport units. These aircraft were already flying in French Moorish troops from Morocco into Spain, and as many as 14,000 were transported in this manner.

During the fall of 1936, France and Russia sent large numbers of aircraft into Spain, so General Franco requested assistance from both Hitler and Mussolini. This request was honored by shipment of the main force of the Legion Kondor, and a parade honored them upon their arrival in Cadiz. Early bombing raids on facilities in Government hands were relatively unsuccessful but did pave the way for the future movements into Poland and elsewhere.

Fighter Group (*Jagdgruppe*) J/88 consisting of three Squadrons (Staffeln) each possessing twelve aircraft constituted the Kondor fighter forces. The bomber force (*Kampfgruppe*) K/88 consisted of four Squadrons of Ju 52 bomber/transports that were notoriously slow and vulnerable. They proved to be effective only in daylight when escorted by large numbers of fighters. Ju 86D bombers that proved to be almost as bad as the Ju 52s augmented these aircraft. Unexpectedly, the air battles turned out to be much more violent than anticipated.

While the war in Spain was at its height, the German aviation industry was beginning to produce modern, high performance aircraft that were intended to become first line unit equipment. In bomber production the He 111 and the Do 17 were considered to be outstanding during test and evaluation and the Messerschmitt Bf 109 single seat fighter proved to be a superior aircraft in every respect for the period. The Ju 87 achieved an excellent reputation because of the general support by General Ernst Udet, an Ace and hero of WWI fame unfortunately, this support caused the premature abandonment of the four-engine strategic bomber development. An accident in a He 70 that killed General Wever, then considered to be one of the best brains in the *Luftwaffe*, killed all chances for the development of a long-range bomber and four engine aircraft were only pushed into development for eventual attacks on shipping.

In 1938, the Kondor Legion began to receive Do 17s that turned out to be eminently successful, leading to the establishment of a special Do 17 unit within the Kondor Legion. These were augmented by large numbers of Ju 87s, which were always operated under a cover of fighter aircraft. This ugly aircraft which always looked as if it was about to pounce, was very slow and non-maneuverable. It was also quite vulnerable, although the slow speed and ability to pull out of a dive at low altitude enabled pilots to accomplish accurate dive bombing attacks. Since the Ju 87 replaced the Henschel Hs 123 biplanes, it could not help but look good to the high command in Germany. Each aircraft was equipped with a siren which emitted a high-pitched scream that was unbearable during the dive phase of each attack, and this, too, lent credence to the reputation of the Ju 87 which extended well into the beginning of WWII.

When fighter units were set up in 1935 or 36, they came under the *Luftgaue* for the purposes of administration, supply and operations. This meant that they were under the control of a province (Gau) within the German nation, and the Province Governor (Gauleiter) was in effect the Commander of the fighter forces. Essentially, the *Luftgaue* organizations concentrated on defense (kind of like the Air National Guard in the United States at the same time) because Germany was afraid that other nations might take military action to interfere with her armament programs that were forbidden by treaties at the end of WWI. Since there were no actual hostilities, it was impossible to evaluate the concept of having fighter aircraft units controlled by geographical commands such as the *Luftgaue* organization.

In maneuvers, bomber formations in peacetime were used most always without fighter escort because the range of single engine fighters did not fit into plans for strategic bombing. Some time between the years 1937 and 1938, it was resolved to build twin-engine fighter units for the purpose of escort. They were called *Zerstörer* (Destroyer) units. In Spain, it was recognized that it was necessary to furnish fighter escort during the day whenever enemy fighter action was to be anticipated. With the introduction of the fast bombers such as the Do 17 and the He 111, the situation did not change. All combatants considered a fighter escort necessary. The Russian and Republican Air Forces always used fighter escorted bomber missions in the daytime.

However, in Germany there was a conflict in operational planning because the Do 17 and He 111s were used in maneuvers while the operational fighters in use then were the Arado 65 and 68, and the Heinkel 51 both of which were old slow fighters. This gave the impression to man that the bombers of the future would always out run the fighters. Experience in Spain with the Bf 109 soon corrected this impression. In fact, this experience should have led to increasing the range of fighter aircraft to the equivalent range of the bombers thus leading to the development of strategic forces, but this step was never taken. It was maintained instead, that the twin-engine fighter destroyer was able to compete on equal or better terms than the single-engine fighter and this consideration eventually had grave consequences.

In Spain, ground attack missions at low level were flown exclusively without fighter escort. If fighter aircraft opposition developed, the Heinkel 51 formations were able to defend themselves, however, these missions usually took place at the same time the Legion Kondor gave indirect cover by flying fighter sweeps in the general area. When operations were conducted against enemy airfields further to the rear from the front lines, a common time over the target was given to both fighter and ground attack units. At no time was actual cover afforded to the ground attack or tactical units.

The crucial turning point in the development of the future *Luftwaffe* came as a result of what could be called no more than a test of weaponry against an undefended town in Spain which had absolutely no military importance, and, as a result, had zero defense. On April 26, 1937, the town of Guernica, a village of 10,000 people became the target of a typical German experiment intended to assess the value of mass bombing from the air. In mid-afternoon that day the Legion Kondor threw every aircraft in commission against this target, beginning with He 51 fighters that bombed and strafed anything that moved both inside and outside the city and then departed in perfect formation.

Following this unprovoked attack, He 111 medium bombers in perfect formation and with great precision bombed from medium altitude wreaking terrible destruction on the collapsing town. After many formations of bombers had passed over the center of the target dropping their lethal loads, the heavy explosive bombs were followed by load after load of thousands of incendiary bombs breaking apart from clustered containers that turned the broken village into a raging fire. The bombs broke all communications, destroyed all transport and completely inundated any ability for fire fighting or rescue the village may have had.

The attack lasted approximately three hours and resulted in the complete destruction of Guernica and the death of 1600 men, women, and children. Not much by today's standards, but in terms of those times, "The raid on Guernica was unparalleled in military history in the form of its execution and the scale of the destruction it wrought." The reaction of the outside world was so intense that it staggered even Franco and his supporters, but it gave little weight to the necessity of or the result of the bombardment. The German propaganda machine had little difficulty over coming the adverse criticism directed at the Legion Kondor as a result of the bombing by denying that any German aircraft ever took part. However, Adolf Galland, who was not in Spain at the time, seemed convinced that the bombing of Guernica was an error caused by primitive bomb sights and inexperienced aircrews, but he was aware that members of the Legion Kondor had a great reluctance to discuss the matter. Eventually, Hermann Göring, during the Nuremberg Trials, had the last word on the subject in 1946. He stated, "Guernica had been a testing ground for the *Luftwaffe*. It was a pity, but we could not do otherwise as we had nowhere else to try out our machines."

There was absolutely no doubt that the *Luftwaffe* gained a tremendous amount of experience in Spain. Since there was no substitute for actual combat experience, many members of the Legion Kondor were able to put their experiences to use when they became high ranking leaders of the *Luftwaffe* when Germany began to conduct its own war. After all a fighter pilot will only find himself when he is up against a real live enemy pilot. If he returns from his first encounter intact, he will be able to meet the next with a confidence that can be gained no other way.

During the Spanish conflict, the Germans experimented with their organizations, operations and equipment as they were developing the techniques that were to become invaluable at the beginning of WW II. For example they abandoned the wing tip to wing tip formations that were used at the time by every other Air Force in the world in favor of the loose pair or "finger four" formations which the United States Army Air Corps eventually adopted at a much later date. They were able to test new aircraft that had not yet gone into production in Germany by flying them under actual combat conditions thus eliminating faults. They were also able to develop new types of aircraft that would prove to be superior to those used by the great powers in years that were ahead.

At the same time there were many lessons in Spain that the *Luftwaffe* missed. Since the enemy in Spain was so inferior, the Germans were able to conduct an air war almost without opposition. The Russian wood and fabric aircraft were no match for the high performance aluminum Bf 109s and the bombers used by the enemy were certainly not up to the standards of the modern German bombardment fleets. Enemy weakness led the Germans to believe that the ground attack by dive-bombers was invincible and invaluable in the role of tactical support, and they concluded that large bomber formations could go to and from targets without fighter escort. Judging from their extremely low combat losses they decided that a low level of pilot training would suffice for the future and they set extremely low aircraft production levels that were based on unrealistic information.

Spain should have inspired the *Luftwaffe* to develop a long range, strategic Air Force, but it did not. Because of their great success in tactical air warfare, only a few men saw the requirement to destroy an enemy industrial capability and none of these men ever became responsible for the development of future aerial warfare concepts in Germany.

CHAPTER TWO

Command and Control

The German Air Force had clearly established air superiority during the Spanish Civil War, but an analysis of intelligence reports revealed that a more aggressive organizational structure would be necessary if the *Luftwaffe* was to expand further. Thus, just before plans were finalized for the first aggressive move into the Sudetenland, all fighter units were transferred from the *Luftgaue* and put under one or another of the Flying Corps (*Fliegerkorps*) along with all sorts of other flying units. This would have been the equivalent of the United States transferring the National Guard flying units to various regular Air Forces by calling them to active duty. The *Luftgaue* no longer controlled the fighter units operationally, but were still responsible for the home basis of various units as well as the small detail of men from each group or wing that were required for house keeping.

The organization of the Corps (Korps) with a General in command was very inflexible because the commander was usually a veteran of World War I who had a younger general staff officer as his deputy. Each Corps contained a number of Divisions called *Fliegerdivision* that included bombers, fighters and other types of aircraft. Each division had a large number of staff people to relieve the Corps of detailed work. Fighter Groups took their orders from the Corps Staff Operations Section along with orders given to bomber, reconnaissance and dive bombing units in the command. Often, a flying leader who was called *Fliegerführer* would assume operational control of aircraft. He was senior commander in the *Korps* because he was usually the Senior Officer although he had no staff. His function was to implement the details even though he had no battle mission plans passed down to him from the *Korps*. All of these organizations relied on the *Luftgaue* for their supply and repair units, so the *Luftgaue* assumed larger areas of responsibility whenever Germany over ran new territories.

This was an awkward organization, with the *Korps*, the Divisions, and the Flying Leaders controlling all different types of aircraft at different levels of command without trying to separate the bombers from the fighters and so forth. This continued until the fall of 1940 when a great organizational change was made by the creation of a Fighter Command in the West and in Germany proper. On the Russian Front the organization stayed essentially the same throughout the war because the role of the *Luftwaffe* as a ground support arm in that theater did not change over the years.

After the campaign in France, the *Luftwaffe* had two Air Forces (*Luftflotte*) stationed in that country for the purpose of attacking England. Since there were no Air Divisions in France at the time, it was necessary to establish special fighter commands under each of these Air Forces because of the concentrated fighter activities during the Battle of Britain. In August 1940, the *Luftwaffe* created the position of Fighter Leader (*Jagdfliegerführer*) for both the Second and Third Air Forces in France, and the name was shortened to *Jafü* for convenience.

At the beginning of the Battle of Britain, fighter operations became so important and so complicated that special operations staffs work loads increased considerably, so the Air Force Commanders found it necessary to give orders directly to the *Jafü* rather than going through previously established channels. Because there was no radar available, there could be no control over the fighter units once they took off, so the fighter leaders had to run the show from the air when the fighter action took place over England proper. During battles, the *Jafü* kept busy planning missions, consulting with Group Commanders, and developing the communications networks that later became the skeleton of the reporting and radar systems. These systems were eventually used in France and the Low Countries since he was out of contact with his airborne forces because they were too far away. In reporting to the Air Force Commanders, the *Jafü* had considerable operational freedom except when it came to controlling aircraft when they were actually over the targets.

After the Battle of Britain in 1941 when the fighter force in the West went on the defensive, many changes had to be made in all fighter organizations. When the Russian campaign began in June, all fighter groups except JG 2 and JG 26 went to the Eastern Front. Air Forces equipped only with bombers stayed in the West because they were almost exclusively engaged in night operations and thus had no need for fighter escort. The Divisions that previously controlled the two fighter units in the West were also sent to the Russian Front, so the *Jafü* took over all control even though the headquarters continued to develop the communications networks.

In the middle of 1941, Radar Control and a Listening Service became available, so it was possible to directly control fighters in the air. This evolutionary change now permitted the *Jafü* to control fighter aircraft directly from the headquarters of an individual group. Each *Jafü* had a representative at Group Headquarters working with the Group Leader to direct operations, but this plan kept the Group Commander from actually leading his unit into combat. Loss of leadership in the air proved to be a disaster and the practice had to be discontinued by shifting control of the fighter units back to the *Jafü* Headquarters once again.

By this time, English night bombing operations in Northwestern Germany forced the enlargement of the German Night Fighter Forces. The 7th Air Force under General Kammhuber, who later became Chief of the new *Luftwaffe* almost a decade after WW II ended, controlled almost all the night fighters located in Holland, Belgium and North West Germany. Rapidly increasing strength of RAF attacks forced the 7th Air Force to develop the best radar and communications networks in all Europe because the capabilities of the night fighting forces had to be improved. In the fall of 1942, when the first American daylight raids penetrated Germany and the low countries, the *Luftwaffe* was forced to organize additional divisions in order to control all the German fighter units in France and elsewhere because this became such a very large and complex task.

As the war expanded, Fighter Divisions based in the Western part of Germany and in France were put under another type of Headquarters called a Fighter Corps (*Jagdkorps*). However, plans to extend this type of control to southern Germany had to be abandoned because there were never enough fighter units on hand to warrant the additional Headquarters. The Corps coordinated the employment of the expanding fighter forces, thus playing a very important role because the Fighter Divisions were only concerned with directing aircraft in the air, so matters of policy and supervision were left to the individual Fighter Corps.

By late 1941, the four Air Forces which formerly divided Germany had moved into occupied territories in order to keep up with changing fronts leaving the defense of the *Reich* to a newly created German Air Force Command for the middle area, the *Luftflotte Reich*. Each of these major units was responsible for a geographical area with Fighter Divisions operating within although the boundaries were changed from time to time. All fighter units in a specific area were controlled operationally by the Division in that area regardless of whether they were equipped for day or night fighting, yet each Division could actually control its own forces if they went outside its borders during a mission. Often, when the fighters exceed radar and communications range, they were passed on to another Division which would be in touch with the aerial situation. This change was always accomplished with great difficulty and proved to be the greatest weakness in the whole Divisional structure. When a Division staff controlling units in the air was faced with trying to accept control of additional units from another Division, there was just too many aircraft and too much combat activity to be handled adequately.

The commander of each Division was a General with World War I background who knew very little about modern fighter aircraft combat, and his Chief of Staff was usually a general staff officer who knew even less. The serious shortage of any general officers that knew anything at all about fighters seriously impaired the efficiency of all the Divisions throughout the war. In addition to a lack of knowledge by those in command Göring frequently replaced commanders without any real reason, so it was virtually impossible to gain experience for this extremely complicated task. Each time an Allied bomber formation completed a mission unscathed, Division Commanders feared for their positions because of Göring's axe. Eventually, was forced by events to promote some of the younger fighter pilots into positions of Division Commanders and these men enjoyed considerable success because of the experience they brought to the job.

Since the Allies were attacking around the clock, all Headquarters had to operate on a 24-hour basis. Every position from the highest to the lowest had to be manned in duplicate or even triplicate because it was impossible for any one individual to be on the job all the time. The absence of a properly qualified Deputy Commander obviously impaired operations, but there was no remedy, since there were just too few fighter pilots with the required qualifications to make good deputies. Neither the C.O., his Chief of Staff, nor any of his subordinates ever flew on operational missions, and, therefore, they had no special insight which would enable them to solve control problems once the fighters were in actual combat.

Division Headquarters varied considerably and those in Germany were the most elaborate. Buildings had to be heavily reinforced to withstand bombing attacks and were usually very well camouflaged. Since the Headquarters was the center of all communications for the Division, each had one or two communications regiments and a senior communications officer, a very important individual who was responsible for several other subordinate units. Communications lines ran to the Division from all airfields, observer corps stations, anti-aircraft units, and to higher headquarters. The installations were all very vulnerable to bombing attacks, and operations were always partially disrupted by communications breakdowns whenever bombs fell anywhere in the vicinity.

When great numbers of aircraft were airborne and in combat, about 150 people were actually involved in the control of aircraft. Division Headquarters had control during daylight operations. Routes of friendly and enemy formations were plotted on a large glass map in a colorful array created by the use of florescent pencils and light projectors. It was necessary to make the entire procedure very exact because so much depended upon accurate position reporting. The fighter control officers (*Jagderleiteroffiziers*) JLO sat at individual desks in front of the map and each were in direct contact with a Squadron or a Group formation in the air. The Division Commander or his substitute sat in front and gave broad directions to various JLO's regarding the disposition of fighters when organizing attacks on heavy bomber formations. These instructions usually stated that a given Squadron was to contact the bombers at a specific point, or that all Squadrons were to be brought up to various conditions of readiness at certain times. The units were expected to follow these instructions when given by the JLO's until they made contact with enemy bomber formations, then the combat leaders in the air took over. The Chief JLO naturally had to do a lot of fast guesswork about where the bombers were heading and what their targets were to be. The Listening Service, which was charged with the responsibility of translating enemy radio transmissions, tried to give the JLO's valuable hints about the disposition and direction of the attacking forces in order to help make the guess work as accurate as possible.

In England, the Allied Air Forces had Control Centers much the same as those in the *Luftwaffe*. However, the plotting boards or maps were horizontal and the airborne aircraft were depicted by "Raid Stands." These stands had tabs showing the estimated number of aircraft, altitude and course, and were pushed along the map by plotters as position reports were relayed from radar stations, from pilots in the air or from the ground observer corps. Usually there was a lag between the time an aircraft was actually spotted and a movement was made with the raid stand, so the controllers were often behind the actual activities in the sky. Much of the actual direction given to airborne aircraft came from controllers of lower ranks at the radar stations because where was very little time delay between observing plots on a radar scope and relaying positions to aircraft in the air. Higher-ranking officers at Wing, Division, or Force levels did not try to interfere except in an emergency.

Since both sides had a Listening Service, a great effort was made by combat leaders to keep radio transmissions between pilots at an absolute minimum. In the USAAF, fighter units often received detailed information in the form of maps from the Listening Service showing from which airfields the *Luftwaffe* had launched strikes against Allied bomber formations. The information usually included which units were involved, number and type of aircraft and routes of attack. Most of this detail came from a combination of radar plots as well as voice transmissions from the enemy and it was generally of great value in predicting what could be expected from the enemy on future missions.

Both sides used daily combat mission reports to analyze missions flown and the GAF Intelligence Organization usually applied this knowledge to give assistance to the JLO's when it came to predicting the possible targets, headings and numbers of aircraft involved in current attacks against Germany. Unfortunately, the Listening Service and the Spoof

Service (an organization charged with putting out spurious orders in English over Allied radio frequencies) could only be controlled from Air Force level, so the JLO's were not able to pull off any special tricks while combat operations were in progress. Galland often tried to change the level of control, but General Martini, Chief of GAF Signals resisted all attempts to invade his empire.

The over all defense system had many faults. It was designed to control all German fighter units efficiently and it did have a positive effect in using all available communications facilities when controlling both day and night fighter forces. However, the system became so complicated that ordinary human mental ability prevented full exploitation of the great potential for tactical and operational control. The JLO's thought they could see what was going on in the air so well that they assumed the role of air strategists, but their lack of experience, coupled with their ground bound position, did not warrant this assumption. They usually failed to consider such vital factors as altitude advantage, visibility, relative strength between enemy and friendly forces, and even the position of the sun. As a result they frequently brought their fighter forces into attacks on enemy aircraft the wrong way and fighter units often found that they were in very bad positions for attacks or, worse yet, were set up for counter attacks by Allied fighters. Still worse, the complexities of the fighter control system made the whole thing seem like a sport to the JLO controllers and they readily lost contact with reality.

Göring, Galland, the GAF Operational Staffs, and the Commanders of the Fighter Corps, Divisions and Air Forces were connected by a telephone system during combat operations. The Division or Divisions over whose territory the air action was taking place would put out a running commentary over this system reporting on the enemy and friendly fighter activities, and this turned out to be a sort of a play by play description of what was actually going on. Any one of the higher commanders (with the exception of Galland, the very person who knew the most and had the greatest amount of experience) could cut into the system to give special orders to the airborne units during missions. These instructions ranged from changing the point at which the German fighters were to attack the enemy bomber streams or to govern the point where the forces were to be massed prior to launching an attack. Radio *Rundfunk*, the German National Radio System, also put out a running commentary, so every German household, in effect, had its own combat situation center. When military communications were damaged or destroyed, the whole round-robin commentary went out over Radio *Rundfunk* in code.

Göring, who followed operations from Karinhall which was in a very remote location or from his town house in Berlin, often interjected silly orders by radio even when there was no way he could be following the air action from either of these two remote points. Adolf Galland made reference to this situation in his book *The First and the Last* as follows:

"This misfortune that had descended on Germany from the air, forced Göring once more to take a greater personal part in the command of the defense of the *Reich*. Occasionally, he assumed the direct command of the fighter units during enemy raids. However, the enthusiasm of the group leaders and at divisional headquarters was not so great when they heard, The *Reich* Marshal is taking over." This was understandable since Göring had once sent all fighters chasing each other as far as Pilsen. The operation went down in the history of Germany's defense as the "Air Raid on Fort Koepenick." An American force had attacked Duren in the Rhineland from above a layer of clouds. The silver paper foils dropped by the bombers had drifted with the wind to the east. While the bombs were already falling on Duren, radar sets picked up the metal strips right up to the Rhine and OP's of the aircraft report service reported strong sounds of plane. The situation was clearly understood by the leading fighter divisions. But their voices carried no weight. Göring was following the approach from Karinhall and considered the situation in the air to be different. For a long time his distrust had spread to the command of the fighter divisions. He assumed that the bombers were flying on in an easterly direction toward Upper Franconia. It seemed to him that a raid on the ball bearing industry of Schweinfurt was imminent, so he ordered all fighter forces into the area. He thought that his fears were soon confirmed because the aircraft report service was now reporting the sound of a large formation flying in the direction of Schweinfurt. Not a bomb fell there. They could not fall, because for some time now the enemy bombers had been on their way home. Fighter Command knew this, but the *Luftwaffe* Commander in Chief believed he knew better than those "nincompoops." Actually what the aircraft report service had announced as enemy formations in the director of Schweinfurt were nothing but our own fighters, flying high above the clouds, directed there by the Fat One in person. Naturally, the fighter force could not locate Schweinfurt because of the clouds. They overshot it in search of the American Bomber Force. The aircraft report service now spoke of strong noises of planes east of Schweinfurt, on an easterly course. This made Göring expect a raid on Leuha. New orders to the fighter force: "All aircraft to proceed in the direction of Leipzig." Here again the same thing happened as at Schweinfurt. Fighter Command gave up trying to convince Göring of the real air situation as a bad job. Again our own fighter force flew over the Leipzig area, but no sign of any air raid.

"By whom, then?" we asked ourselves.

"What are the Americans up to?" Göring at Karinhall asked himself. A new idea: The Skoda works near Pilsen is probably the target. So the fighters were sent as far as Pilsen chasing themselves because of the sound of the aircraft report service and because of Göring's judgment and evaluation of the air situation. It was a happy coincidence that the cloud cover slowly broke up and we could see the sky full of German fighter planes, but no sign of enemy bombers. As the sun broke through over Pilsen, Göring suddenly realized that he had been backing the wrong horse. He took it with a sense of humor, knowing that he had made a fool of himself. He sent a telegram to all commanders and leaders of the units concerned in which he congratulated himself and all participants with engaging irony of the "successful defeat of the air raid on the Fortress of Koepenick."

The broad principles of tactical employment of fighter aircraft were formulated in doctrines issued by the German Air Force Headquarters Staff and by Göring himself. Instructions for attacking Allied bombers before they dropped their bombs, concentration of the fighter forces on one Allied raid per day, and the regulations involving more than one mission per day were typical of the orders sent out only by the highest command level. The Corps and Divisions usually expanded on these directives, varying them to meet local requirements. The General of the Fighter Forces was expected to augment all directives with greater detail by outlining the technicalities involved in each type of mission to be flown.

Tactical regulations were passed on to the Fighter Groups after they had been checked by the GAF Headquarters Staff or sometimes even by Göring. The Fighter Divisions on the ground had complete authority to control formations in the air and this policy really subordinated the battle freedom of the formation leaders. If there had been enough good pilots to fill ground positions, the system probably would have been more successful. However, most of the JLO's were pilots who were unfit for further combat, or, at the least, very good communications officers who were able to grasp something of the idea of aerial combat.

Galland, himself remembered many occasions when the Division Headquarters Staff broke down completely, and operations had to be shifted to some lower group headquarters with limited facilities. Even under these more difficult circumstances, the results were as good if not better than they always were. The ground bound fighter control officers were far too rigid in exercising detailed control of routes, altitudes and points of attack for the airborne formations. This was especially true when they tried to avoid contact with Allied fighters, yet bring the German fighters into the attacking bomber stream at the right time and place. Fighter formation leaders were not allowed to take the initiative, so serious errors were often committed as mechanical or communications failures developed within a Division Headquarters. Frequently, the fighters missed the attacking bombers altogether. Rigid control was necessary, however, at night and during the day when bad weather prevented pilots from seeing the ground while trying to orient themselves. The Divisions used shadowing aircraft to follow the attacking bomber stream, and their crews reported good verbal pictures of the air situation which included weather, cloud cover, altitudes of enemy formations and so forth. After the early part of 1944, however, the use of shadowing aircraft had to be stopped because they suffered heavy losses from the numerically superior Allied fighter escort. As a result the Division JLO's had even greater difficulties in grasping the air situation.

The Ardennes Offensive in December 1944 forced a rather radical change in the fighter aircraft organizational structure. Since almost all of the remaining German fighter units were situated along the Rhine River at this time, an organization called Air Force Commando West was organized to command all the GAF units in that sector. Fighter Corps II had almost all the fighter ground attack aircraft in Germany under its command, but had no units capable of combating Allied heavy bomber attacks. To remedy this, ground attack fighter groups were controlled by Fighter Corps II when they flew ground support missions for the Army in the West. For missions against heavy bombers, the control was switched to an experienced air to air combat command, Fighter Corps I that then issued operational orders. This change over was accomplished by flashing the code words, "Defense of the *Reich*." This situation proved to be unsatisfactory because Fighter Corps I did not understand or appreciate the disastrous operational conditions the German Army was encountering on the ground in the West and often took fighters away from absolutely necessary ground-support missions. Worse still, the fighter forces would be spread out all over Germany after each mission against the Allied heavy bomber attacks, and their parent unit Fighter Corps I was unable to reassemble them fast enough to make new attacks when additional missions of heavy bombers penetrated Germany.

In late 1944, the *Luftwaffe* decided to change from this detailed form of control to give more initiative to the Fighter Groups. A mission with the code name of "Big Blow" was to be the last one to use rigidly controlled fighters. It was the largest attack made in force by the *Luftwaffe* and it was directed at Allied air bases from Brussels to Eindhoven. It took place on the 1st of January 1945. Ten Fighter Wings were briefed the night before for a massive attack on all Allied airfields in Belgium and France. Using the cover of low altitude, the pilots were instructed to use cannon, machine guns, and light bombs against any kind of target they could find on the ground. Altogether 650 Fw 190s, 45 Bf 109s and a few Me 262s were involved though the German public was led to believe there were over two thousand fighter aircraft airborne on the mission. Göring, himself, visited many of the bases before the fighters took off in hopes that he would give the departing pilots inspiration. The weather for the day was icy and cold, but the propaganda organization gave the mission very complete photographic coverage anyway since this was to be the last mass take-off of German fighter aircraft for the duration of the war. Because the attack was to be made at low level, the Germans realized that navigation would be difficult, so the huge formation of fighters was led to the various targets by three Ju 188's. Over three hundred aircraft flew over the Zuider Zee, heading for Brussels and a second formation passed over Arnheim on the way to Eindhoven, while a third passed over Venlo on the way to American forward bases. The surprise was complete. At Brussels-Evere hundreds of Allied aircraft were parked wing to wing where they were easy targets for attacking German pilots. Hangars were set afire and personnel seeking shelter were mowed down indiscriminately. Although a few Allied fighters succeeded in taking off, others ran into enemy fire and either crashed, burned or exploded before they could become airborne. Anti-aircraft fire brought down many German aircraft but, in spite of these losses, over one hundred Allied aircraft were destroyed on the ground at just that one location.

At Eindhoven, the destruction was equally complete even though an RAF artillery spotting Taylorcraft Auster pilot radioed that he had just observed a formation of at least 200 *Messerschmitts* flying low on a course of 320 degrees. Again, a few Spitfires and Tempests managed to become airborne but in spite of their efforts, a complete Typhoon and a complete Spitfire Wing were destroyed on the ground.

When the German aircraft still in a condition to fly returned to their bases, *Luftwaffe* officials estimated that one hundred aircraft had fallen in combat, either to enemy fighters or to anti-aircraft weapons. Many aircraft that did manage to return to their bases were damaged beyond repair. Galland realistically estimated that the total number lost on this mission was over three hundred aircraft and pilots. Regardless of the high losses suffered by the Allies, they were able to make limited patrols over the area for the following week and, by the end of that time, all units were back up to strength again. For that one week of grace, the *Luftwaffe* had sacrificed all available fighter aircraft reserves, including night fighters and the sky was even more wide open than before for heavy, medium and light bomber attacks that were striking into the heart of Germany proper.

After the "Big Blow" and during the Ardennes offensive, the Fighter Groups actually put out their own commentaries and gave orders to formations in the air from their own headquarters. This practice continued throughout the remaining months of the war. Even in defense of the *Reich*, formation leaders were allowed much more freedom to pick out their own courses, and to decide when to attack. However, by this time, the fighter arm was so weakened and disorganized, suffering from all kinds of shortages, that it was almost impossible to judge the results of this more independent policy. Still the formation leaders demonstrated a new aggressiveness when they were given the responsibility of finding and destroying Allied bombers with a minimum amount of interference from the ground.

CHAPTER THREE

Politics Rules

German civil Aviation had come into being in 1917 so immediately after World War I ended uncomfortable military aircraft were being used inside Germany for regular air service. When the war ended Hugo Junkers had founded his own airline which flew into various cities inside Germany as well as to most of the major cities in Central Europe. With the revival of popular interest in aviation in the 1920 to 1930 time period, more than 30 different independent airline operators had entered into the air transport field because it was an unexpectedly profitable business. However, it was tremendously over populated so, one by one, the various independents were forced into bankruptcy while still others became incorporated into one large airline, the *Deutsche Aerolloyd* with only one rival, Hugo Junkers. In 1926 Junkers finally joined his only rival which then became *Deutsche Lufthansa*, the state monopoly airline.

Behind the scenes, many ex military airmen were secretly using the facade of Lufthansa to select important positions in German civil aviation in order to insure the future development of military projects while they were in civilian disguise. One of these men, Erhard Milch was to become the top ranking German air officer beside Hermann Göring who fell into Allied hands at the end of World War II. His testimony provided great insight into the problems that befell the *Luftwaffe* during the air war over Europe.

Milch was an ambitious man who had been a pilot in the Great War and had subsequently been the factory manager of the Junkers Company prior to being given the job as first Managing Director of Lufthansa. This was the first step on what proved to be a fast direct rise to power as a dominating military personality. While working closely with the German Central Government, Milch had gradually built up a reserve of trained airmen over the years by incorporating lectures and practical instruction into the Lufthansa training programs that were of great value from a military point of view. As a result a surprising number of men who had led fighter and bomber formations into battle in 1939 had been transferred from civil aviation just before the outbreak of war.

Although there had been a proliferation of various types of civilian aircraft developed in Germany from 1930 onward, the nation lacked the ability to provide over all planning and guidance to develop machines that could be adapted to military missions. In order to improve the administration of all the different types of civilian aircraft that were to be the nucleus of the new German Air Force, a secret technical department was established within the new German Air Force. Known as "C-Amt" this organization was made up chiefly of engineers and officers transferred from the Central Government who had been friends of Hermann Göring since the end of the war in 1918. Erhard Milch, with an excellent reputation as the energetic Chairman of Lufthansa, was made the Deputy Air Minister of this new department. Another man also assigned to the technical department was Ernst Udet, who had been a reckless fighter pilot during the Great War, a flying acrobat of the early twenties and a film stunt man in the early thirties. Udet had always disliked working for anyone but himself because he had no ability as an executive. A brief career as an aircraft industrialist had ended in disaster for him, but his great popularity and skill as a flyer convinced Göring that Germany needed this practical man who possessed great imagination. Udet finally agreed upon an assignment, but insisted that he be given no official status. He did not want to wear a uniform again, nor did he desire to enter the dangerous whirlpool of Nazi politics.

On a trip to the United States as a representative of the *Luftwaffe*, Udet had been shown a new weapon, the Curtis Dive-bomber, an aircraft that could dive from a great height onto a selected target and then climb away. When Udet returned from America, he was convinced that the dive-bomber was of the utmost importance for Germany. He was able to co-erce Göring to buy two new Curtis Dive-Bombers even though Milch objected. As an Oberst in the technical department, Udet was able to use his influence to draw up specifications for an aircraft to be used as a dive-bomber using the Curtis machine as a starting point. The first air craft to be built to fulfill this objective was the Henschel 123 with which Germany entered the Spanish Revolutionary War.

In the winter of 1936, General Wever, who had been a vociferous advocate of the long range strategic bomber had died and those who followed him considered this type of machine to be a luxury Germany could not afford. In addition, the new Blitzkrieg techniques required a large force of twin engine medium bombers that would be massed behind a spearhead of dive-bombers, so production priority was given to the Ju 87, which was a brainchild of Udet.

However, Erhard Milch was the one man in the higher echelons of the *Luftwaffe* who bitterly resented Udet's popularity that had followed the success of his dive-bomber brainchild. At the time the German air-craft industry was rapidly expanding toward a war time production basis, and Milch, who had established himself as a brilliant organizer seemed to be long over due for promotion. He did not know that certain of his colleagues were working against him and he soon discovered that instead of a higher position, Göring was gradually divesting him of the power he already had achieved by relieving him of various routine but important matters. Then Udet was appointed director of the technical side of C-Amt to become responsible for future aircraft production, Milch who knew quite well that the uninhibited one time fighter ace was totally unsuitable for this responsible task, became his considerable opponent. Despite the apparent success of the Junkers Ju 87, Milch suspected that the excite-ment over the Stuka, which was then raging like a cyclone through *Luftwaffe* Headquarters, was misplaced, and he, blamed Udet for leading Göring astray. Milch was appalled that such a man could have been pro-moted over his head because it seemed to him that Göring could not have made a more unsuitable choice. But for some time Göring who had been suspicious of Milch and remembering his reputation as an ambitious or-ganizer, had decided it was time to replace him with someone less likely to covet his throne. While it was likely that Milch, who had openly criti-cized Göring on more than one occasion, hoped to thrust his commander out of office. This was almost impossible because the higher ranks of the *Luftwaffe* were always seething with intrigues aimed at destroying any man whose ability might lead to rapid promotion. Never the less, Milch, Udet, and another capable individual named Loerzer hurriedly prepared for war.

From the beginning, Erhard Milch and Ernst Udet had been convinced that light and medium bombers should provide the nucleus of the German Air Force and these two men were largely responsible for the concentration on a few basic types of aircraft which were being produced in large numbers. About this time, Göring appointed General Hans Jeschonnek to the position of Chief of Staff of the *Luftwaffe*. This man also felt that the dive-bomber was the most suitable weapon for the *Luftwaffe* and soon after he took office, he issued instructions that all new aircraft under construction or slated for production must be able to dive bomb. When Germany actually attacked Norway and Denmark successfully, much of the credit for this operation was due to the well organized planning and excellent *Luftwaffe* organization at the time Milch was in charge. He had arrived at Oslo on the 16th of April to assume command of the new *Luftflotte* 5, a new air fleet headquarters established to control all air operations in Norway. Three weeks later he returned to Germany to supervise preparations for a western offensive. This was the only time Milch left his desk in Berlin to undertake a command in the field. He clearly demonstrated that he was an administrative genius whose abilities were wasted outside the main *Luftwaffe* Headquarters because neither Udet nor Jeschonnek were capable of grasping the vast potential of air power as Milch did.

By October 1940, Ernst Udet had become disillusioned because he had come in between Erhard Milch and Jeschonnek who had completely different ideas regarding the development of aircraft. Göring attempted to persuade him to cooperate with both men in order to keep up the facade that there were no internal problems within the *Luftwaffe*. He found this impossible to do and on the night of November 17th he shot himself. Later, Erhard Milch received Udet's mother at the Kaiserhof Hotel in Berlin and blandly gave his version of the accident involving a weapon so secret that the details could not be revealed. Milch then assumed Udet's responsibilities in the Technical Department.

In 1941 Hitler was convinced that the war against Russia was won and he wanted to build up the Air Force in preparation for the defeat of England. Milch, as Chief of the Technical Department, recognized the priorities of this decision and knew he must work closely with Dr. Todt of the Labor Organization as well as Albert Speer then the Chief of Armaments Construction. On February 13th, Milch who had by that time been promoted to the position of State Secretary of the Air Ministry, held a meeting with the armaments chiefs of the various branches of the services and representatives of the armaments industry. Because of the difficulties caused by the conflicting demands of the three services, the Economics Minister Funk proposed in the meeting that Milch become the one man who would make all final decisions in assignment of priorities because of his relationship with Göring who controlled the four-year plan.

Speer, who had anticipated this power play, had arranged with Hitler before hand, that the people present would be called before Hitler to hear first hand that Speer would be the ultimate authority in decisions of priority. Speer later recalled, "That same evening, I had a full discussion with Milch who pledged an end to the rivalry the Air Force had hitherto practiced toward the Army and Navy in matters of procurements. Especially during the early months his (Milch's) advice became indispensable; so out of our official relationship there grew a cordial friendship which lasted to the present." On February 15th, Field Marshal Milch, General Thomas and General Olbricht as General Fromm's representative visited Hitler to tell him of the plans for the future that were formulated as a result of the February 13th meeting. None of this sat well with Göring who felt that he should have been in total charge.

Later in the fall of 1942, Speer, Milch and Fromm (Army) had agreed upon and issued the following statement, "Our feelings tell us that this year we are facing the decisive turning point in our history. Speer added, "the turning point was impending, with the encirclement of the 6th Army at Stalingrad, the annihilation of the Africa Corps, the successful Allied land operation in North Africa and the first massive air raids on German cities. We had also reached a turning point in our wartime economy for until autumn of 1941 the economic leadership had been basing its policies on short wars with long stretches of quiet in between. Now the permanent war was beginning."

In the latter part of November 1942, when it became obvious that the 6th Army was encircled at Stalingrad, Hitler had asked Göring about the possibility of supplying Stalingrad by air. Göring had personally guaranteed that this could be done in spite of the fact that the Air Force General Staff had determined that supplying the pocket by air was impossible. In December the airlift got underway, flying into four airfields within the pocket. It had been determined that 300 tons of supplies were the minimum needed to sustain the encircled force. However, aircraft after aircraft crashed on arrival in the Stalingrad ring and the airfields soon became clogged with wrecks. The Fw 200 and the He 117s proved to be particularly unsuitable due to maintenance problems and a lack of experienced aircrews. However, in spite of this hopeless situation Hitler signed a special decree giving Field Marshal Milch the power to take all measures necessary for supplying Stalingrad this without Göring's permission.

Milch arrived in Russia full of confidence because of the figures of transports supposedly available to General von Richthofen's transport fleet. However, the facts were different. Only one third of the number he had been given were serviceable and only about 100 aircraft were actually in flying condition. Milch immediately returned to Berlin where he was able to locate another 300 aircraft, but only once did Richthofen's fleet come close to the target of 300 tons when 154 aircraft managed to fly 289 tons of food and ammunition in to the pocket. The daily average of 100 tons was nothing more than a starvation ration for the beleaguered garrison. By the 2nd of January, the Soviets had captured all the remaining airfields and the 6th Army was doomed. The *Luftwaffe* lost 536 transport aircraft, over 100 fighters, and 2,200 aircrews.

Milch faced yet another air transport debacle. By March of 1943, the Afrika Korps was trapped between the Allied 1st and 8th Armies and General Erwin Rommel was pleading desperately for gasoline and all other supplies so regardless of the overwhelming Allied air cover, the *Luftwaffe* again had to fly in supplies to encircle troops. Day after day, loaded Ju 52s and Me 323s staggered into the air out of Sicilian airfields to meet their destruction. In one single month 200 air transports were shot down because they lacked fighter cover.

As General Galland so aptly commented, "The performance of the air transport crews was beyond praise. Even if they succeeded in getting their planes with the urgently required load safely into the cauldron, they were exposed to uninterrupted bombing and low level attacks while refueling and unloading. The devastating decimation of the *Luftwaffe* on such forced missions was nothing new, but here, because of the extended duration, we used up the very substance of our air force."

By this time Jeschonneck and Milch were looking everywhere and in every theater for fighters that did not exist. In Tunisia only two fighter groups survived and these were in danger of being eliminated if the battle continued. Milch did try to augment the close support capability with the new Henschel 129 dive-bomber and the giant Me 323 troop carrier, but these were swallowed up also and did little to effect the outcome of the battle. The British 7th Armored Division entered Tunis on 7 May 1943 and the battle was ended. The Allies had eliminated the *Luftwaffe* from the skies in the Mediterranean Theater. Although 200 bombers bad been operational at the beginning of the campaign, only 40 remained in action and these were later shot down in strikes against Malta and other heavily defended targets.

By this time, Milch and Albert Speer were becoming an increasing threat to Hermann Göring whose leadership of the *Luftwaffe*, had been severely criticized by Hitler. Since the entire hierarchy of the German government was rife with jealousies, undercutting and back stabbing, Milch and Speer tried desperately to get Göring into a frame of mind where he would actively participate in a plan to usurp Martin Bormann's increasing power and influence over Hitler. The mechanism to be used was to force Bormann to reveal truthful labor statistics instead of grossly exaggerated figures that would please Hitler. Speer had set the stage by demanding an additional 2.2 million workers for the total work force. The confrontation took place in a building that had been erected near Berchtesgaden to house the Berlin Chancellery Secretariat.

As Speer was to write later, "Milch and I expected that Göring would ask Sauckel (Bormann's representative) for explanations and make him change his labor assignment policy. Instead, to our horror, Göring began with a violent attack on Milch and thus indirectly on me. It was outrageous that Milch was making so many difficulties", he said. "Our good party comrade Sauckel who was exerting himself to the utmost had achieved such successes. He at any rate felt a great debt of gratitude was owed toward him. Milch was simply blind to Sauckel's achievements. "The conference proved to be a total failure."

Later Göring confided in Speer, "I know you like to work closely with my State Secretary Milch. In all friendship, I'd like to warn you against him. He's unreliable; as soon as his own interests are questioned, he'll trample over his best friends." Speer immediately passed this remark on to Milch who laughingly said, "A few days ago Göring told me exactly the same thing about you." Further, a few days after the conference ended, Milch commented that Göring had taken the position he did because the Gestapo had proof of his drug addiction. Some time before Milch had suggested to Speer that he look closely at Göring's pupils. Speer recalled later that he had been told by his attorney that Milch had been an addict before 1933. In addition, it was later learned that Bormann had made Göring a gift of six million Marks from the industrialists Adolf Hitler Fund.

As another insight into the corruption that was rife inside Germany just before the Allied invasion, Speer, Milch and many other titans of government were invited to a gala birthday celebration for Göring at his palatial estate, Karinhall. Naturally; all guests were expected to bring expensive gifts which ranged from gold bars to valuable paintings and sculptures. Fink delivered the birthday speech lauding Göring's abilities, qualities, and attributes and all the dignitaries toasted him as one of the greatest Germans.

After dinner, Milch and Speer discussed where the money came from for such opulence. Milch recalled that Göring's old friend Loerzer who had been a famous fighter pilot during World War I had sent him a carload of stuff from the Italian Black Market consisting of women's stockings, perfume and other rare items. Loerzer had informed Milch that he could have these items sold on the black market and had even included a price list with the shipment in order to keep black market prices uniform throughout Germany. The great profit that Milch could realize from the sale had already been computed. Instead, Milch had distributed the goods to employees of his ministry. Many other car loads had also been sold to benefit Göring and the Superintendent of the *Reich* Air Ministry who carried out the sales for Göring had been transferred out from under Milch's control and had been assigned directly to Göring. Milch also was aware that larger amounts of money were transferred from the Air Ministry General Fund directly into Göring's personal account. Although these amounts of money were great, they could only cover a small portion of Göring's enormous expenditures, and it was obvious that he also received great additional sums from industry representatives who provided him with subsidies.

Shortly after Göring's birthday party, Speer fell ill and was confined to a hospital where Milch visited him on February 23,1944. By this time the American Eighth and Fifteenth Air Forces were concentrating their bombing on the German aircraft industry with a result that aircraft production had fallen to one third of what it had been. At the time, the Ministry of Armaments had successfully dealt with the extensive bomb damage in the Ruhr area. So Milch proposed that a Fighter Aircraft Staff be formed that would combine the talents of the Air Ministry and the Ministry of Armaments in an effort to over come the crisis in aircraft production. Göring was violently opposed to this proposal because it would appear to weaken his authority, but Hitler thought the idea had merit, and appointed Karl Sauer, the Director of the Technical Department to this new position. Milch favored Sauer for this appointment although Sauer's power seemed to be growing at Speer's expense.

Partially because of his illness and partially because of his erosion of power, Speer intended to hand in his resignation to Hitler toward the latter part of April 1944. Not only did representatives of industry come to the hospital to plead with him but late at night on April 20th, Field Marshal Milch, Karl Sauer and Dr. Frank called upon him to bring a verbal message of confidence from Hitler. Although this message had more or less been exhorted from Hitler by Milch, it did convey love and esteem. Speer fended off arguments that he should remain at his post for a long time but eventually his three visitors prevailed upon him.

On May 12, 1944, the American Eighth Air Force struck at several fuel plants in central and eastern Germany beginning a new phase of the air war that could only result in the end of German armaments production. At Speer's insistence, Göring, Keitel, and Milch, together with four leading industrialists were called to discuss this crisis at Obersalzberg Göring and Keitel tried to down play the situation with generalities, but Hitler insisted on evaluating the circumstances in objective terms. Although 16 days later production had been almost restored, both the Eighth and Fifteenth Air Forces struck again on May 28th and 29th, and fuel production was reduced by one half. Milch again played an important part in representing the *Luftwaffe* by frankly presenting the plight of the fuel industry although Göring wanted to hide the facts from Hitler because he felt he would be blamed. By this time, Milch had become Göring's opponent.

Although work on jet engines had been conducted as early as 1941, and preparations had been made for large scale production of the Me 262, preparations were proceeding slowly, so General Adolf Galland made an impassioned plea to step up this effort. At the end of April 1944, Galland, in a resume of the air battle situation commented in part, "In the last ten battles we have lost an average of more than fifty aircraft and forty men. That means five hundred aircraft and four hundred airmen in ten great raids and at the present time they cannot be replaced. We need higher performance to give our own fighter force a feeling of superiority even if we are inferior in numbers. For example, to give some idea of values: at the moment I would rather have one Me 262 than five Bf 109s!"

Almost six months before on the 26th of November 1943, the Me 262 had been demonstrated before Hitler at Insterburg in East Prussia. The *Führer* asked at the time, Can this aircraft carry bombs?" Professor Messerschmitt had replied at the time, "Yes, my *Führer*, theoretically, yes, there is enough spare power to carry 1,000 lbs, perhaps even 2,000 lbs."

Hitler had replied, "For years I have demanded from the *Luftwaffe* a fast bomber which can reach its target in spite of enemy defense; in this aircraft you present to me as a fighter plane, I see the *Blitz* Bomber with which I will repel the invasion in the first and weakest phase. Regardless of the enemy air umbrella, it will strike the recently landed mass of material and troops creating panic, death and destruction. At last this is the Blitz Bomber! Of course, none of you thought of that?"

Now, a conference held in the summer of 1944, again at Obersalzburg. Hitler again mentioned the Me 262. "How many have been produced so far!" he had demanded. At the time Milch replied, "One hundred and twenty, my *Führer*."

Hitler asked, "And how many of these can carry bombs?" "None, my *Führer*" Milch had answered, "The Me 262 is being produced exclusively as a fighter aircraft."

As it was reported later, the words Milch spoke exploded in Hitler's ears like a succession of firecrackers. Two minutes later Hitler was on his feet, hammering with his fists on the table and roaring insults and wild accusations. "You have constantly lied to me and deceived me! The

Luftwaffe is disobedient, unreliable and disloyal. Look at all the promises! And yet what has it achieved? Nothing! My orders have been systematically disobeyed. I will not stand it any longer!" Stunned by the tirade, Milch had been unable to find his voice and in the background Göring had nodded agreement with everything Hitler said. Soon afterwards, Milch was stripped of all his authority and became like so many others who had briefly confronted Hitler.

With the exception of Göring, Milch was the most senior representative of the *Luftwaffe* to be interrogated by the Allies at the end of World War II. He had perhaps had more contact with both Göring and Hitler than any other *Luftwaffe* General, and certainly had more technical experience and background than any other *Luftwaffe* member. In his book, *Inside the Third Reich*, Albert Speer consistently referred to Milch with respect and indicated that he was a friend. Undoubtedly, Milch had the organizational and technical background for his ultimate appointment as a Field Marshal, and his insight into the problems facing Germany and the *Luftwaffe* toward the end of the war could have been of remarkable assistance to Hitler had that man been capable of listening. Milch's contribution to these interrogations was great.

CHAPTER FOUR

The Men

Adolf Galland

Anyone who has ever been a student of the *Luftwaffe* or of World War II, will be familiar with the name, Adolf Galland. He was, beyond doubt, one of the most spectacular and outstanding airmen to emerge from the defeat of Germany and his book, *The First and the Last,* is a brilliant description of the rise and fall of the German Fighter Forces of the years 1938-1945. He made a great contribution to the interrogations obtained by the Allies at the end of the war.

Adolf Galland, was born in Westerholt, Westphalia. His father was bailiff to the Graf von Westerholt, a post that successive heads of his family had held since 1742 when the first Galland, a Huguenot, had immigrated to Westphalia from France. Galland began his aeronautical career at 17, flying gliders at Borkengerge, a heath near Westerholt.

In 1933, after a successful tour of gliding, Galland was admitted to an airline pilot training school in Brunswick. Joining the then unofficial *Luftwaffe*, he was secretly trained in Italy in 1913. Although a crash during a training flight in Germany severely injured one eye, Galland managed to memorize an eye chart, pass a physical examination, and continue flying.

In 1937 Galland volunteered for service in the Kondor Legion, the name for the German Volunteer Corps serving with Francisco Franco's forces in the Spanish civil war. He sailed from Hamburg with 370 other German soldiers, garbed in civilian clothes, masquerading as a "Strength Through Joy" tourist group. In Spain he was assigned to a fighter squadron near Vittoria on the Northern Front. Galland wore the uniform of a Spanish Captain, customary with pilots of the Kondor Legion. His baptism of fire came in June 1937, when he engaged Loyalist fighters in a Heinkel He 51 fighter. Although *Messerschmitt* Bf 109s had been introduced in Spain, a few flights still used the slower He 51s. These planes were no match for the Curtis and Rata fighters of the Loyalists and it was Galland's policy to avoid dogfights with the enemy so his activities were restricted to the strafing of ground targets. In Spain the Germans learned a great deal about ground support operations. Galland firmly believes that the Russians, who used close support most effectively in World War II, copied the techniques first used by the Kondor Legion.

Galland was recalled to Germany in the summer of 1938. He had flown over 300 sorties in Spain. The command of his flight was taken over by Werner Mölders, who was destined to become one of Germany's leading Aces in World War II. Shortly before the end of the Spanish Civil War, Mölders became the youngest Wing Commander in the *Luftwaffe*. In Germany Galland was assigned to a desk job in the Air Ministry. His work consisted of working out directives for the organization and training of fighter pilots for ground support operations. He detested the work and longed to return to flying duties. His first task was to organize and equip two new fighter groups. This was accomplished at record speed, but not without certain sacrifices in the quality of training and equipment. Many of the pilots wore insufficiently instructed in the operation of their new aircraft and the planes themselves old He 51s, Me 123s and Me 45s, were hardly the last word in performance.

These new fighter groups were created to support the imminent occupation of the Czechoslovakian Sudetenland. On September 29, 1938, however, the Munich Pact eliminated the need for their immediate use. On August 23, 1939, the German-Soviet Non-Aggression Pact was signed. The invasion of Poland became only a matter of time. On September 1, 1939, Galland who had joined a ground support unit, was at an airfield at Reichenau in Silesia. In the darkness preceding dawn he took off with his squadron. World War II had begun.

The collapse of the Polish armies is now history. The Polish Air Force was destroyed on the ground. Communications were bombed out of existence. Transport was halted by strafing operations and the Polish troops wore demoralized by the Ju 87 Stukas. In 27 days the war was over and the Polish Army capitulated. Warsaw was in flames. The Red Army had rumbled to the Bug River.

Galland, who had flown over two sorties a day during the campaign, was awarded the Iron Cross, Second Class. On October 1, 1939, he was promoted to *Hauptmann* (Captain). Shortly afterward he was reassigned to a fighter unit, *Jagdgeschwader* 27, at Krefeld. The stage was set for the battle in the West. Galland began his documentary of what followed in his book.

Because of the easy campaigns in the air in Spain and the Polish campaign, Hitler and the *Oberkommando Wehrmacht* came to the early and wrong conclusion that the *Luftwaffe* would suffer limited losses in the air in the future. As a result, prior to the invasion of Russia, there were no long ranged plans for any acceleration of pilot training. When the campaign in Russia began to falter early in 1943, every effort was made to increase the flow of pilots to operational units, but training took time and time was really running out for the German Air Force.

By the middle of 1943, there was not only a shortage of pilots, but there was also a shortage of aircraft, aviation fuel and experienced maintenance personnel. In combat, the more experienced pilots seemed to survive while the pilots who had just graduated from flying training were generally the ones who did not come back from missions. This situation persisted regardless of the amount of training a student received in flying school. Since all of these factors became increasingly important in the early part of 1944 just before the invasion, the German Air Force was placed in a squeeze from which there was no relief.

Initially, pilots were selected just for basic flying training, not for special branches of the *Luftwaffe*. Organizations charged with the selection of pilots lacked coordination, had no specific guidelines, and did not work at all together. Although the *Oberkommando Wermacht* regulated the quotas of personnel to be assigned to the Army, Navy, and Air Force as well as the SS, the Navy and the SS had the most success in recruiting. The Hitler Youth, USFK (older boy's glider training schools) and the flying schools did not cooperate with each other. In general, recruits who were to be trained as fighter pilots came from allotted quotas levied on various youth groups. The training system of the NSPK (an organization which gave some young men a limited pre-flying and pre-military training) volunteers from various operational units and volunteers from other branches of the *Wehrmacht* such as the Army and the Navy. When these transfers took place the volunteers had to be replaced by men transferred back out of the receiving units.

Flying personnel for all branches of the *Luftwaffe* were assigned to the Office of the Chief of GAF Training to be trained at various primary and basic training schools. In basic school, pupils were selected for specialized training as a prelude to assignment to fighters, ground attack, bombers and so forth, but the Fighter Arm considered the selection process to be abysmally bad. In the GAF the bomber pilot was thought to be the most important of all branches because of the great demands made upon him and historically the bomber pilot had been given the most responsibility in Spain, Poland and the low countries. During the Blitzkrieg, Hitler had counted on the bomber pilot to bring about the collapse of the British Government. In 1944 however, it was finally recognized that there was an even greater physical and mental demand on the fighter pilot when any attempt was made to stop the increasingly heavy bomber attacks on the homeland.

Most of the above average and gifted pilots, especially those who were considered to be of officer material, were assigned to the bomber arm. The *Luftwaffe* leaders believed that any pilot who was not suitable for anything else would be a satisfactory fighter pilot. Since there were very few staff officers or instructors with fighter pilot background who could be spared from combat to fulfill the needs of the school system, the requirements for pilots for the fighter arm were not specifically answered. These requests were badly represented when they were discussed at all.

In 1944, because of the reversals of the aerial war, this philosophy underwent a change, but until then the supply of fighter pilots who reached operational training units was found to be unsatisfactory because they did not meet the high physical and mental demands of the time. For several reasons, pilots were seldom discharged from the operational training units when they actually lacked flying ability. In the first place, the demand for fighter pilots at the front line units kept growing steadily even though the demand could never be met. In the second place, the GAF could not afford to ground students who had been given a great number of hours of air training because the investment of fuel, already in very short supply, was entirely too great to be ignored. Even though there was such a great demand for qualified pilots, many students who were graduated from flying schools were unsatisfactory or were even complete failures, but only about ten percent were actually fired from operational training units because they were unsuitable.

Early in 1944, this situation did begin to improve because many of the branches of the GAF were not required for combat. Large numbers of bomber, reconnaissance and transport pilots were examined at a re-evaluation center and were selected for fighter training. Successful candidates were strong, tough and resilient with good vision who were not over twenty-seven years old. The most desirable were front line pilots with experience, men who had strong character, were mentally capable of bearing up under great pressure, and who took visible pleasure in fighting in the air.

Galland, by then the *General der Jagdflieger*, always believed that the fighter arm was the place for capable and intelligent men because the greatest demands were made on fighter pilots since they always fought alone. From 1944 on, the Chief of Flying Training used these principles of selection for fighter pilots and the training program became completely successful. However, this was possible only because the other branches of the GAF were no longer able to use large numbers of newly trained pilots. In general, the fighter pilot requirements as Galland saw them were that the best candidate would volunteer, be physically and mentally tough, possess courage, be aggressive, have fast reactions, have excellent vision, be of firm character, and have excellent morals.

Galland often tried to develop an ideal fighter training program which could have been attained providing all the necessary training facilities and fuel were at the disposal of the fighter forces during the war. Unfortunately, his plans never materialized because Hitler insisted that England be kept under aerial attack and the fighter forces even suffered at the very height of the heavy bomber attacks on Germany because even the most modern aircraft had to be equipped to carry bombs.

Galland felt the rules used for selecting fighter pilots early in 1944 were more than adequate except that pilots from other branches of the GAF should not have been accepted. He believed that candidates should come from rural areas such as the mountains, the farms and the sea shores, because he felt that city life had an adverse affect on the nervous systems of young men. He also believed that ability in sports was of great significance.

In his interrogations, Galland outlined what he believed would be an ideal fighter pilot training program for the future. When he was 17 years old, the young pilot candidate would get supervised training in sports, physical culture, gliding (towed and stunt), theoretical training in meteorology, navigation, aerodynamics, and aeronautical engines. Each young man would be trained to shoot with hand weapons and skeet shooting would be a must. After induction, the cadet would get four months of basic training that would teach him military discipline and further his knowledge of elementary flying subjects.

Specialization would begin immediately, and all aspects of training would be designed to enhance the fighter pilot outlook. Elements of flying and training would be divided into two stages, basic flying and instrument training. Aerobatics, air to ground gunnery, attack tactics both with single aircraft and in formation with others, fighter against fighter using gun camera film, navigation and cross-country flying would all be a part of the curriculum. All commanding officers and instructors in the training units would have operational fighter aircraft experience. From twenty to twenty five percent of the trainees would be eliminated during this phase.

In Elementary Flying Schools, students would be trained on both single- and twin-engine aircraft so they would learn the feel of heavier machines. In this part of training lasting eight months, each student would get about 100 hours of instruction which would include about 20 hours flying with an instructor. In addition, there would be a one-month course on instrument flying covering about 50 hours of blind flying, bad weather operations, fighter control procedures and radio navigation. Graduates of this school would receive a certificate for single engine aircraft with moderate landing speeds.

Upon completion of Elementary School, students would be sent to a Fighter Training School that would last for 6 months and would include 100 flying hours. In this school all of the instructors would also be experienced combat fighter pilots. Flight Surgeons with experience in combat units would be on hand to determine who was not physically or mentally suited for combat. In this phase another 20-25% of the students would be eliminated because they would be below acceptable standards. Students would be trained on older single and dual seat combat fighter aircraft and the school would use all sorts of training aids for aerial gunnery and navigation. Organized sports would be stressed and students would be given extensive practice in the use of hand weapons.

In this phase, pilots would gradually be converted to single engine fighters from two-seaters and they would be allowed to train solo until they had mastered the unit aircraft. There would be adequate training in Squadron strength with both open and closed formations. Closed formations would be used for show and for flying discipline but not for actual combat training that would be conducted at high altitudes instead of low levels as the GAF always did. For gunnery practice each pilot would make 12 runs on ground targets which would be mock-ups of enemy aircraft. Six runs on a sleeve target or an aircraft in the air and twenty sorties of fighter against fighter or fighter against bomber using gun cameras would be flown so the attacks could be evaluated. These exercises would be conducted by elements of two, four, and twelve aircraft all equipped with both computing and fixed gun sights.

In addition, there would be extensive navigation and cross-country flights, mock battles between single aircraft and between units as large as twelve with plenty of mock attacks against bomber formations. For dive bombing practice, at least five runs would be required while carrying rockets and another five while carrying bombs. In these advance schools, daring and rough flying would be encouraged, and the resulting increase in accident rates would be acceptable because the German Fighter Force had been on the defensive so long that it was beginning to lose *esprit de corps*.

After leaving the Fighter School, each pilot would spend at least two months in an Operational Training Unit that would culminate his training. He would then be assigned to a front line combat unit. In the OTU, the instructors would be the best and most experienced fighter pilots with special teaching abilities. They would all have demonstrated a high degree of capability in leadership. Each pilot would fly 60 hours in the OTU and every hour would be spent in training flights that were reproductions of real operations based on the latest front line experience. Only the most modern aircraft would be used because the pilots would be sent to units using these types. Very few men would be eliminated at this stage because by this time they would all be good fighter pilots. During this last phase of training, instructions would be given in all the latest developments of aircraft, engines, communications equipment, enemy tactics, and enemy material. Students would fly missions against captured enemy aircraft that would be flown by other German pilots. Each Operational Training Unit would be attached to a Wing or a number of Wings so that the operational units would be able to draw on a number of qualified instructors. They would also be able to receive replacement pilots who had been trained by their own people under conditions that would be found on the front.

In general, the philosophy of Fighter Command was such that it was not necessary to make all pilots officers. The GAF conception of an officer was a man so talented that he would need extra duties and responsibilities in order to keep busy. If this was not the case, officer rank could become an inducement for an individual to seek flying status. Late in the war, in General Galland's Me 262 unit, there were too many officers and it became difficult to keep discipline even though all of them had additional duty responsibilities. Galland, himself, felt that perhaps a rich nation could afford to commission all pilots, but Germany had too few men with the educational requirements such as 12 years of schooling necessary for officer rank. Galland thought that training should be both physically and mentally grueling in order to prepare men for the hardships of war, but he recommended letting his pilots blow off steam in their spare time with liquor, sports and women. Apparently, there were little if any bad effects from this policy

Heinz Bär

There were, of course, instances where Galland's philosophy regarding the merits of achieving officer rank did not apply. One such case concerned Lt.Col. Heinz Bär who became the eighth ranking ace of the *Luftwaffe* with a total of 220 aerial victories to his credit. His comments made a major contribution to the Intelligence Reports that were generated by the Allies ar Kaufbeuren at the end of the war.

Bär was born in Sommerfield near Leipzig May 25, 1913. As a youth he was given instruction in gliders, and in 1930 graduated to powered aircraft to obtain his private pilot's license. He had an ambition to become a commercial pilot for Lufthansa, but this required three different kinds of pilot's licenses at the time in Germany. Because he was the son of a farmer and because of the depression years, he was unable to afford civilian flying instruction, like many young men in Germany, he decided to join the *Luftwaffe*. He had hoped to acquire the necessary flying time and licenses as he trained in the service, and then leave to join Lufthansa. By 1938, he was a sergeant pilot flying fighters as the threat of a European war increased, so there was no chance that he could be released from the service to join Lufthansa.

When the war actually broke out and Sergeant Bär actually went into combat, he scored his first victory on the 25th of September 1939 by shooting down a French piloted Curtis P-36. As the war unfolded, he flew in the Battle of France and the Battle of Britain in a JG 51, emerging from the latter conflict with seventeen victories to his credit.

Trevor Constable and Colonel Raymond F. Toliver recalled a part of Bär's conflicts with the British in their book, *Horrido!,* which is about the fighter aces of the *Luftwaffe*.

"When the Bf 109 pilots first tangled with the Spitfires and Hurricanes, German pilots generally were instructed to dogfight with them. This was a traditional carry over from the First World War. The Germans soon learned that the Spitfire and Hurricane could out-turn the Bf 109 and after heavy losses the German pilots were instructed to hit and run. Bär was one of the *Luftwaffe* pilots who tried time and again and learned the hard way that a Bf 109 does not get into a turning battle with a Spitfire. On numerous occasions he got the worst of his encounters with the formidable British fighter. Six times he was barely able to stagger back to France in his shot up Bf 109. On the seventh occasion he was not so lucky.

On 2 September 1940 he was grinding back across the English coast with an over heated engine, his Bf 109 riddled and perforated in both fuselage and wings. A lone Spitfire pilot bounced the staggering cripple and administered the coup de grace. The would-be Lufthansa pilot bailed out just before his machine plunged into the Channel within sight of Dover. An exhausting swim of nearly two hours brought him to one of the Channel buoys shortly before dusk. A German patrol boat on its evening rounds later plucked Bär from the drink. He was flying the next day. Bär was transferred to Russia shortly there after as a First Lieutenant and a Squadron Leader. There with JG 51 he managed to shoot down 43 enemy aircraft in less than two months. He had clearly demonstrated that he was not only an ace but also a leader. He downed five Russian aircraft on 30 June 1941 and topped this one-day effort by shooting down six more on the 5th of August 1941. On the 31st of August he was shot down and forced to bail out of his aircraft. Upon hitting the ground heavily, his parachute dragged him along the ground for several hundred yards fracturing his spine in two places. In spite of his injuries, he managed to spend two days and two nights hiking and hiding until he reached the German lines."

He returned to the Eastern Front after a long period of hospitalization and by the middle of February 1942 was credited with ninety victories and was awarded the Swords to go with his Knight's Cross with Oak Leaves he had been awarded in August of 1941. Between this time and the end of the war Bär destroyed six more Soviet aircraft as well as 107 aircraft of the Western Allies. He left the Eastern Front in the spring of 1942 and was assigned as Commander of JG 77, a unit heavily involved in efforts to capture Malta from the air. He also flew in North Africa until Germany was driven out of Tunisia and was successively the Commander of JG 1 and JG 3 while flying continually in combat. Between 1939 and 1945, he was shot down 18 times, parachuting four times and belly landing in pastures, grain fields and emergency landing strips fourteen times.

In January 1945 Bär became commander of the German Jet Fighter School at Techfield, near Augsburg. As a consequence he was not in jet combat until very late in the war. However, he did achieve sixteen confirmed kills in the Me 262 becoming the leading jet ace of the period. Some of the sixteen kills were in a Me 262 equipped with a rocket engine from the Me 163 in addition to the two jet engines. This special aircraft had a rate of climb of nine to ten thousand meters in three minutes which was roughly ten thousand feet per minute at a speed of 750 kph. He was able to down a British Mosquito on his first mission with this aircraft. Bär was appointed to command JV 44 the elite "Squadron of Experts" when Galland was wounded and Luetzow was killed on 22 April 1944. By the end of the war his experience in aerial combat was longer and more diverse than any other *Luftwaffe* leaders. He flew more than one thousand missions and encountered almost every type of Allied fighter on all fronts.

Again to quote the book, *Horrido!*, Bär told Col. Raymond Toliver his opinion of Allied pilots and aircraft encountered during the war:

"Combat against American and British fighters was a highly varied thing and pilot quality was the great imponderable factor until combat was actually joined. In general, the P-38 Lightnings were not difficult at all. They were easy to outmaneuver and were generally a sure kill. The P-47 Thunderbolt could absorb an astounding amount of lead. These aircraft had to be handled very carefully in combat because of the large number of hits they could take with no seeming impairment of their performance.

The P-51 Mustang was perhaps the most difficult of all Allied fighters to meet in combat. The Mustang was fast, maneuverable, hard to see, and difficult to identify because it resembled the Bf 109 closely in the air. These are my general impressions of Allied aircraft and of course the quality of the Spitfire needs no elaboration. They shot me down once and caused me at least six forced landings. A very good pilot in any of these aircraft was tough to handle and if he had the tactical advantage he had a good chance to win the fight. You see from my own eighteen experiences as someone else's victory that they often did win. But when we got the Me 262s it was a different story, and they were at a tremendous disadvantage against us.

The jet was just too much against a single propeller-driven aircraft. We could accept or refuse combat with the Allied fighters. It was our choice. The edge in performance and armament given us by the Me 262 was decisive in fighter combat.

This assumes, of course, that the Me 262 was functioning correctly on both engines. In the jets we were in real trouble if we lost one engine and it was a petrifying experience also to be low on fuel, preparing to land, and find that Allied fighters had followed you home."

Bär was an extremely handsome man with chiseled features and a straight, hawk like nose which-made him look every inch like a hero. He had an excellent sense of humor, an outgoing personality and a ready wit, all of which undoubtedly came into play as a commander. Others insisted that he was a natural born leader and it was widely known that he would never ask others to do anything that he had not first done himself. He had all the ingredients that Galland looked for in fighter pilots and suffered the same fate that others did at the end of the war. Considered to be a militarist, he had great difficulty finding employment. However, in 1950 he was placed in charge of engine powered aircraft in the German Aero Club, supervising sport flying in West Germany. He enjoyed this activity because it put him back in the flying business.

On the 28th of April 1957 he was demonstrating a light aircraft in Brunswick. The machine spun out from 150 feet and plunged into the ground killing Bär in front of his entire family. With over one thousand missions during which he destroyed 220 enemy aircraft, it had to be fate that brought him to an untimely end twelve years later in an aircraft designed for safe sport flying.

Gordon M. Gollob

When Adolf Galland was relieved from the position of *General der Jagdflieger* January 1, 1945, he was replaced by Colonel Gordon Gollob, who was perhaps one of the least known men who held the Knight's Cross with Swords and Diamonds. Born in Austria, Gollob became a fighter instructor as a Lieutenant in the Austrian Air Arm in 1936. He had been trained long before the start of World War II at the same time as Adolph Galland and Werner Mölders. He was made a *Zerstörer* pilot with ZG 76 in 1939 and destroyed his first enemy aircraft in Poland in that year. In April 1940, he became a Squadron Commander in ZG 76 and took part in the Norwegian campaign during that period.

During the Battle of Britain, Gollob was transferred to JG 3 on the English Channel and became the commander when this unit was transferred to Russia in January 1941. He was returned to Germany on December 1941 on a temporary assignment to the Rechlin Test Center where he clearly displayed great talent for developmental work in fighter aviation. He later returned to the Russian Front as Commander of JG 77 in May of 1942 and his *Geschwader* became singularly successful on the southern part of the Eastern Front until September 1942. He became the tenth German fighter pilot to score 100 victories and on August 29th 1942 he became Germany's leading ace with 150 victories. On October 18,

1941 he alone shot down 9 enemy aircraft while losing only one wing-man which is a considerable feat in any Air Force.

He was again transferred to the Western Front in October 1942 to become *Jafu* 5, or Fighter Leader 5, in the West, a position that lasted until April 1944. It was obvious by this time that he was destined for greater things and eventually became a member of the fighter staff under the leadership of Saur in the Ministry of Armaments. His special technical skills made him very valuable in the testing of novel aircraft, and he made very substantial contributions to progress on the operational side of many modern fighter aircraft projects. In 1944, he led the fighter staff for the Battle of the Bulge even though his responsibilities during this period kept him away from fighter combat operations.

When Galland was dismissed as General of the fighter Arm at the end of January 1945, Gordon Gollob became his replacement. He not only survived the war but made an important contribution to the intelligence reports that were the basis of this book. He flew 340 missions and downed 150 enemy aircraft included 6 flown by pilots from the West. However, he occupies a much more important position in the history of the *Luftwaffe* than his awards or victories suggest because of his important contributions to superior aircraft and armaments.

Walther Dahl

Colonel Walther Dahl was born in Lug/Rheinpfalz on the 27th of March 1916. He, too, learned to fly through the same schools that were available to young men in Germany who had this ambition. His route toward success as a fighter pilot was slightly different than most of the others in that he began his career as a *Geschwader* adjutant with JG 3 in 1940. His first victory was achieved on the Russian Front in June 1941. He fought in Russia with JG 3 as Commander from July 1943 to May 1944, and then became involved with a Wing that had been formed especially to fight the USAAF daylight bomber formations.

This Wing was the famous *Gefechtsverband* that consisted of pilots who were out to prove themselves or who had been given a last chance because of inferior performance on one occasion or another. It could have been considered almost a suicide Wing because inferior pilots were almost herded into the heavy bomber formations at great loss to the *Luftwaffe*. The Wing was initially called JG zbV and was a derivative of the *Wilde Sau* Wings (Wild Boar) that had achieved great success both day and night with desperation tactics. Eventually, the Wing OAS called JG 300 and two ramming groups were included in the organization Equipped with long nosed Fw 190s the unit was known as the Ram Fighters (*Rammjägers*)

Here again, this unit had spectacular success against the four engine bomber formations. The object of each attack was to close in to point blank range before firing, and if all else failed to ram a bomber in hopes that it would be brought down but the German pilot would either bail out or manage to land his damaged aircraft successfully. Dahl himself was eminently successful with these tactics, eventually becoming the third ranking German ace in regard to the number of four engine bombers brought down when he reached a total of 36. Altogether he flew a total of 600 missions while destroying 128 enemy aircraft of which 77 were Russian including 25 over Stalingrad. He was eventually appointed to the position of Inspector of Day Fighters on January 26, 1945 and remained in that position until the war ended. He, too, made a major contribution to these interrogations. In March 1945 the third ranking German Ace Günther Rall who had accumulated a total of 275 victories was made the Commander of JG 300 which was then operating from a base near Salzburg. Shortages of gasoline and inadequate facilities continually reduced the fighting power of JG 300, so when Americans were reported to be rolling down the Autobahn, Rall disbanded JG 300.

CHAPTER FIVE

Morale

In most military organizations morale is a constant concern to the command level. A winning team will have few problems associated with morale, but continuous reversals and high losses can seriously disrupt morale and affect fighting spirit. This was the case in the *Luftwaffe* by 1944. Prior to that year periodic leaves or rests away from the combat zone were a must for flyers involved in daily combat activities. In Germany various fighter units had initially organized their own rest homes locally, and it was necessary to do the same in occupied countries because it was either too far or too difficult to travel back to the home land in the short time that was allowed for leave. In 1942 Galland had proposed to Göring that a central rest home be established for fighter pilots, and a *Jagdfliegerholungsheim* (fighter pilot rest home) was established at Wiesse, south of Munich, at a cost of about one hundred thousand marks. In 1944 all other rest homes maintained by various groups and wings were dissolved because of the shortage of help.

The rest home was a place for pilots whose nerves and physical condition needed improvement, but it was not a convalescent institution for wounded pilots, since anything that could give it a medical atmosphere had to be avoided. A visit to a rest home was voluntary although each wing had a certain quota of pilots to send, and the Commander and Medical Officer in each unit decided who needed a rest. Galland's office allocated the quotas since he was General of the Fighter Arm, but the Wings were allowed to deal directly with the rest home without going through channels.

The home could accommodate about one hundred men at a time of all ranks and ages although it was not generally used by the older men who preferred to take their leave in a large city. By 1943 the younger fighter pilots rarely lived long enough to become exhausted to the point where they needed the home to rest. Since the proportion of officers to enlisted men to be assigned to the home was the same as that in the combat units, the home was not the exclusive property of officers. The atmosphere was informal, and all sports including hunting, fishing, mountain climbing, and swimming were encouraged. Wine and special foods were liberally supplied by flying units in France and Italy, and by local politicians, so the food was excellent and plentiful.

Women were not allowed to stay at the home because there would be the usual problems stirred up by rivalry and by jealousy between wives and sweethearts. However, the moral aspect of female companionship troubled no one and many complaints were received from local authorities about the wild life in the home. Respectable women and wives stayed in rooms in resort hotels nearby or in homes in the vicinity that were held open for this purpose. The bomber pilots had a similar home across the lake from the fighter home, and wives and sweethearts were allowed to live there. Unfortunately, the high casualty rate soon turned the place into a home for widows and orphans, and the home lost its original purpose. Eventually, the high casualties among fighter pilots changed the atmosphere too as more and more wounded and recovered pilots suffered nervous collapses and were sent there. The home always had a few rooms available for visiting fliers who found themselves in the vicinity, and this contributed to the club-like atmosphere. In addition, the home was used for important conferences of the *Luftgaue*, *Jagdkorps*, and *Jagddivision* personnel. In general the home had a very beneficial effect in repairing the nerves of many pilots, and it improved the *esprit de corps* of the Fighter Forces as a whole.

In regard to rest homes, the Allies were faced with similar problems and arrived at slightly different solutions. In England most of the members of the Royal Air Force, with the exception of the French, Polish, Belgian, and other nationalities, had their homes somewhere in the British Isles. Since England is relatively small, most servicemen could go home on leave to visit their families. In the USAAF it was impossible to visit home during a tour of duty, so the American Red Cross established rest homes for combat crews.

In general these homes were rented from titled landowners, and were located far away from areas that could become targets for enemy bombers. The normal visit to a rest home was two weeks, and a great effort was made during that period to provide as much of a civilian atmosphere as possible under the circumstances. Flyers were allowed to wear civilian clothing that was provided for them by the home (it was illegal to wear anything but a uniform during wartime in the service). There were Red Cross women, both young and old, to provide the touch of mixed sexes, food was excellent, and there was an abundance of sporting activities available.

In contrast to the *Luftwaffe* rest homes, aircrews always outnumbered the resident staff in the Red Cross homes, and it was against regulations to bring in women from the outside so there were no problems of jealousy created by the presence of women. All meals were delightful affairs with the women providing stimulating conversation. Often dances were held to the accompaniment of phonograph music, and current motion pictures were shown whenever they were available. The British civilians living nearby often invited various members of the USAAF to visit them in their homes, and often contributed horses so that aircrews so inclined could ride on occasion.

Also in contrast to the *Luftwaffe*, the USAAF had individual homes for fighter and bomber pilots as well as enlisted aircrews. It had been concluded that the personalities of these individuals might differ widely, especially under conditions of stress, so efforts were made to provide an atmosphere with as little a potential for friction as possible. Since most of the homes were located in remote areas, the surrounding countryside was beautiful and most relaxing.

In the *Luftwaffe* each officer, noncommissioned officer and enlisted man was allowed 14 days leave per year, and additional leaves of up to eight days including travel time were often granted. Only the Wing Commanders could grant leaves to Group and Squadron C. O.'s although mass leaves were sometimes granted when a unit was being transferred from one front to another or when a unit was being re-equipped in Germany.

Generally, the men spent their leaves at their own homes because of the short traveling distance involved no matter where the units were stationed. There were no special leave privileges granted to flying personnel even though there was no such thing as a tour of duty, but, often, medical leaves were granted when a pilot had flown a certain number of missions for the purpose of rest and recuperation. Usually, the Medical Officer with the approval of the Commanding Officer would grant this type of leave that could last as long as four weeks. However, the Unit Commander was often forced to reduce the leave period because of the pilot shortage.

Whenever there were great emergencies in special campaigns such as the French Campaign in 1940, the Battle of Britain, or the start of the Russian Campaign in June 1941, all leaves were canceled or, at the very least, definite limited leave quotas were established. From time to time leaves were canceled during Defense of the *Reich* because of the limited number of personnel and the operational urgency of aerial battles. The Fighter Force was never able to establish a program of relieving pilots after they had accomplished a certain number of missions since there were never enough pilots. As it was, pilots flew until they were shot down, injured or killed, or until the war ended.

In the USAAF leave policies were liberal although there was no opportunity for an individual to return to the United States while on leave during his tour of duty. As the war progressed, however, an individual who volunteered for a second tour of duty after having completed the requisite number of missions was often allowed to visit the United States for a 30 day period of rest and recuperation. It was quite possible to finish a tour of duty in a very short time, and pilots who did so were either given non-combat assignments in the theater or sent back to the U.S. to train others. In England it was a general practice to take leave either in London or in coastal cities. Many organizations rented apartments or flats, especially in London, and the aircrews rotated through them on an individual basis. In addition, there were several inexpensive billets provided by the Red Cross where crews could spend time in a club like atmosphere. Officially, there was no effort to provide any diversions such as woman companionship and it was up to the individual to find fruitful ways to spend his leave time.

Early in the war the German Air Force had special service units that visited the operational units and gave much pleasure to the troops. Sport, entertainment, and relaxation facilities were readily supplied, and propaganda companies showed films and produced plays. As the war progressed and the over-all situation took various turns for the worse, manpower and transportation problems made it necessary to reduce this activity until the grimness of the air war eliminated it completely in 1944.

The *Luftwaffe* tried to be democratic as far as recreation was concerned, so officers were not allowed to monopolize the attentions of visiting actresses and all performances had to be put on in front of all ranks including mechanics. Unit clubs were open to all flying personnel, both officer and enlisted, and there were clubs for ground crews as well. Officers and enlisted pilots always ate together due to an order issued by Göring. Club life was fairly uncontrolled, but German law for the duration of the war forbade dancing, so it was not attempted except rarely in very private circles. The men drank whatever was available in the country where they were stationed, and, since France and Italy accounted for much of the fighter activity, there was plenty of wine. Hard liquor was simply not available. In the fighter arm drinking was the cause of most all of the disciplinary problems, and drunkenness was discouraged, although it happened frequently. Women were not allowed in the clubs for security reasons in Germany as well as in other countries.

On the Allied side, most of the American Fighter units were stationed at temporary air bases, although a few had occupied permanent Royal Air Force establishments. The early arrivals in both Bomber and Fighter Commands got the best facilities and the rest had to make do with Quonset Huts and temporary barracks. In general, the Service Clubs were of the same quality as the rest of the base installations. Officer's Clubs were generally in Quonset Huts, and usually they featured a bar, lounge, and dining room with rather Spartan accommodations. Usually the food was adequate, no better or no worse than that served to the Allied forces in general. Hard liquor for bars was a matter of local purchase, and the American practice of issuing a combat ration of alcoholic beverage when the pilots returned from each mission assured a supply.

Often, aircrews would contribute to the general fund in a club in order to help the Club Officer provide extra niceties. Many of the clubs featured slot machines and the proceeds were used to provide extra benefits. Although the clubs were meeting places, especially at mealtime, many of the operational Squadrons had mess facilities within the Squadron area, and aircrews often preferred to eat with their mates rather than trek some distance to the central club. This happened more frequently when the weather was bad because most airbases had unpaved paths and roadways that turned muddy when it rained.

Generally, the Clubs tried to arrange social events in which women participated whenever it was possible. Often dances were held featuring bands made up of musically inclined members of the unit involved. Nurses from nearby base hospitals were always invited, as were Red Cross Workers who generally toured the vicinity in Clubmobiles. Many of the officers invited young ladies from local communities, and some of the more daring would import girlfriends from London or some of the other larger cities. Most of these affairs were genteel although there were always rumors of wild parties at this or that airbase. Americans in general seemed to treat women with more consideration and respect than did their English counterparts, and so most dances were conducted with decorum.

The Royal Air Force generally occupied the better airbases because they were there first. These bases featured large hangars, brick buildings, and excellent service club facilities. Usually the officer's clubs were of excellent modern design for the period, and there were living quarters built into the facility. The RAF Clubs had anterooms, lounges, messing facilities and bars, and the presence of numbers of Batmen (enlisted men who were servants to the officers) who ran the facilities provided service, which was generally excellent.

The British had a completely different concept of decorum when women were present than did the Americans. On the other hand, Americans stood aghast at the actions of their counterparts at stag affairs in the clubs. A "Dining In Night" in a Royal Air Force Mess usually provided visiting Americans with a great number of surprises. After a formal toast to the Royal Family, formally dressed members of the Mess and their guests sat down to a table suitably set with RAF crested utensils and dinnerware. With no smoking allowed, the meal would begin with subdued conversation. Usually at some point one individual would take exception to a comment made by another and would toss a bun at the offender. From then on pandemonium would result. The air would be filled with flying buns, butter or whatever came to hand. Ribald laughter and suitable insults were the order of the day until the "Smoking Lamp" was lit and members adjourned to the lounge or bar for further action.

After that, RAF games would begin. Most of these games resembled American football or European Soccer, and often injuries resulted. Members of the Mess sang all sorts of songs, some dirty and others quite lovely, and there was generally some sort of action taking place throughout the club. On one occasion members of the mess set fire to a stack of newspapers in the middle of the lounge and then threw furniture on top of the fire. When this was extinguished by the club custodians, an effort was made to move the grand piano in the lounge out through the front door of the club in order to throw it into the reflecting pool in the driveway. When the door proved to be too small for the piano, the members made it wider with a sledgehammer and then successfully threw the piano into the pool. The activity stopped when someone set off a tear gas bomb in the middle of the building and emptied the place.

In many of the messes there were footprints across the ceilings in the dining rooms though often the ceilings were thirty feet high. It was explained that the members of the mess would form pyramids until the last climber could be supported upside down with his feet touching the ceiling. He would then walk upside down with lamp black on his shoes in order to put the footprints in the proper places. To Americans this kind of activity was unbelievable because there would have been heavy punishment meted out for actions such as these at American Clubs. In RAF Clubs, however, nothing seemed to happen. In the case of the grand piano, it was fished out of the pool the next day, the front door of the club was repaired, and the club was cleaned up good as new. This sort of thing was chalked up by the authorities, to youthful exuberance.

With the *Luftwaffe*, brothels were set up in occupied territories, supposedly as a method of control for venereal disease, and the GAF personnel used them freely. There was one type for officers and another for enlisted men in uniform and still another for enlisted men in civilian clothes. The only brothels set up for the exclusive use of the *Luftwaffe* which were not open to any of the other services existed in Russia and were set up in 1943 by General von Richthofen. The *Luftwaffe* recruited local talent for these institutions. Brothels were not a problem in Africa because heat and hard work kept ambition under control. Galland believed that the use of these military brothels did not minimize VD, but did minimize homosexuality which had always been a problem in Germany.

Promotions were always of great concern for the *Luftwaffe* because they had such a great bearing on morale. Promotional policies were the same with the fighter arm as with other branches of the Air Force except that fighter pilots initially received more promotions for bravery than did the other branches. In any case, the time in grade was usually much longer than that in other Air Forces throughout the world.

Noncommissioned officer pilots usually left the fighter schools with the rank of UFFZ (Unteroffizier) which would be the equivalent of Warrant Officer in the U.S. Military; however, front line units complained that this rank should be given only to pilots who were ready for combat. Pilots not ready for combat went to operational units with the rank of *Gefrieter* or *Obergefrieter* (the equivalent of Airman 1st Class) and were promoted to UFFZ when they had proven themselves in combat. NCO's could be promoted by Group Commanders or the Wing Commodores although each Squadron Table of Organization called for five officers and 11 *Oberfeldwebels* (Master Sergeants). Each NCO was required to spend one year in grade, but promotions for bravery could be given out freely by the Commodore.

Officers were divided into three classes: Active, Reserve, and *Kriegs* (Irregulars). Active officers were trained as pilots in special flying schools and then continued training in the regular fighter schools. These men received commissions when they left the *Luftkriegschulen*. *Kriegs* Officers were either selected and trained as officer candidates after they became NCO's or those who passed special examinations entered the GAF as officer candidates. From the start of the war no active officers were commissioned, but *Kriegsoffiziers* could become active by passing special tests and signing up for military duty for life. Great stress was always placed on political reliability and often politically desirable officer candidates who could not be spared from operational units would receive commissions without going to the *Luftkriegschule*. In fact, Göring often appeared in operational units to make spot promotions of NCO's to officer ranks with little or no reason for his actions. As a result the GAF was burdened with many unqualified officers.

Early in the war a requirement for officer rank was successful completion of a course in a Gymnasium or higher school which was the equivalent of a U.S. prep school or high school. Later this requirement was reduced to eight years education, which was the amount usually given to all German youth. Galland did not believe that all pilots should be officers because the German ideal of an officer was a man who was given special privileges and extra duties commensurate with his superior abilities. In an ordinary GAF fighter unit there were not enough extra duties to keep more than five officers happy and busy, hence each Squadron was staffed with five and usually fewer.

Officers of the three lowest ranks were given the same opportunity for promotion whether they were *Kriegs* or *Aktiv,* but Reserves were not promoted as rapidly. Active officers were given preference for promotion above the rank of Major. Usually officers were promoted to higher grades because they held a position calling for advancement, but Galland thought it would have been better to have dual ranks, one based on seniority and the other based on position. In this way a young officer could have the pay and honor of higher rank if he had the ability, and still would not be promoted too fast. He could be given a special title that would go with his position, such as *Kommodore* or *Kommandeur.* However, promotions were usually made on the basis of seniority, and position on the seniority list was determined by grades the individual received on the officer candidate examinations and later from his fitness and efficiency reports.

Before a man could be promoted, his superior officer had to certify his political reliability as a National Socialist, but poor endorsements were rare and good endorsements were almost automatic. Many able young men were promoted very rapidly early in the war, but many lacked leadership ability so this practice eventually was discontinued.

American Air Forces had essentially the same problems regarding promotions at the time, but there was no requirement to establish any sort of political reliability. Regular officers and graduates of the military academies had promotional preference prior to the war but the tremendous influx of personnel made it necessary to promote on the basis of performance because there was always a need for higher ranks as the force expanded. Due to the considerable losses in the bomber units, promotions often came rapidly to those men capable of handling them effectively. Although this situation existed in fighter units too, the losses were not quite so high and promotions did not come quite as rapidly.

In general bomber pilots in the USAAF were sent back to the United States after completing 25 missions unless they individually requested either an extension of tour or an additional mission allocation. Fighter pilots who completed 100 missions were either sent back to the U.S. or given non-combat assignments or administrative jobs. Requests for additional missions or for an additional tour were more frequent in the fighter forces, and pilots would often only log combat missions if they had actually encountered enemy aircraft, so the number of combat missions showing in their records would remain low.

Obviously, when a Major or Lieutenant Colonel Squadron Commander was sent back to the United States, it was necessary to replace him with another Major or Lieutenant Colonel. Often the new Commander would have received rapid promotion to his rank by virtue of seniority or superiority. When he was transferred, the next in command would be given his position and would receive the promotion as soon as the paper work was completed. Perhaps the record for promotion was achieved by one officer who went from Aviation Cadet in flying school to full Colonel in 31 months. However, this man was a brilliant individual who eventually became a four star General before he retired.

Although promotions and promotional policies had a lot to do with morale in the GAF, policies for awarding decorations also had a great bearing on *esprit de corps*. Valor was such a desirable attribute that there were almost no disciplinary problems in the fighter arm that could have been charged to mutiny, desertion, or cowardice. Early in the war most of the higher decorations were given out by Hitler and Göring, and this was considered to be a singular honor. In the beginning it was very hard to earn the Iron Cross, Second Class or First Class, but, as the war progressed, these medals were given out for one and five victories, respectively. Initially, the Knight's Cross was intended to be Germany's highest decoration, but eventually Hitler added new dimensions by creating the addition of Oak Leaves, Swords and Diamonds.

Among German Fighter Pilot's the Knight's Cross was without a doubt the most sought after military decoration. Many ambitious young pilots were killed in combat because of an insatiable desire to win this award, and many others who had accumulated almost enough victories to qualify threw all caution to the winds only to suffer death at this critical stage. The award of the Knight's Cross to a fighter, night fighter or *Zerstörer* pilot was recognition of a substantial degree of superior skill and fighting spirit. When he had at last become eligible, it was apparent to all that the pilot selected had flown his aircraft on hundreds of missions in deadly combat against numerically superior enemies and had still been able to achieve more than average success.

Since the fighter pilot's ultimate objective is to shoot down an enemy aircraft, it would have been easy to make awards based on this criteria alone. Greatly different fighting conditions in various theaters of operations changed so frequently during the five years that Germany was at war that it became necessary to evaluate each single victory so that all the imponderables of luck, chance, and opportunity could be considered in making recommendations for awards. Since a pilot's success could be measured in figures such as the number of aircraft destroyed, the number of missions flown or even the number of combat hours involved, a pilot with a desire to achieve could do so purely on the basis of numbers.

Many individuals who had received the Knight's Cross had a vast number of enemy kills over the years, so it appeared that there were no rigid requirements specified in regulations, and, in fact, there were no absolute instructions that awarded the Knight's Cross for a certain number of enemy aircraft destroyed. The High Command of the *Luftwaffe* established certain limits and then tried to stay within them. Guidance procedures were issued to Commanders in the field, but there were deviations both upward and downward from the standards and a certain number of kills was by no means a guarantee of the Knight's Cross.

Prior to the German invasion of Russia, criteria for the award was a simple matter because fighting conditions were the same for all pilots. The Knight's Cross was awarded for 20 victories and this was the same figure that had been established during World War I for the award of pour le Merite, the highest award of that period. Usually the Knight's Cross was presented immediately after this number of victories had been achieved, but deviations could be made based on special circumstances such as heroism in fighter bomber or fighter escort operations since the general leadership and the unit success as a whole had to be taken into consideration. Because this medal was awarded to a limited number of pilots, the Commander in Chief of the *Luftwaffe* often personally intervened in both approvals and disapproval's, so from May 1940 to May 1941 a total of only 35 fighter and six destroyer pilots were decorated with the Knight's Cross.

When the Germans invaded Russia, the German fighter pilots shot down so many Russian aircraft that using the old standards for the award of the Knight's Cross would have led to a devaluation of the medal. From June 1941 on, there was a steady increase in both victories and awards, and in the entire year of 1941, 62 fighter, five-night fighter, and 10 destroyer pilots were awarded the Knight's Cross. An increase in the requirements was then directed by the High Command and the change was made from 25 victories required in June to 30 required in September, and then to 40 in November at which time the increase in requirements stopped. At that time the difference in difficulty of fighter combat between the various theaters of war became a severe problem when it came to evaluation. It was much easier to achieve a victory in Russia because the aircraft were technically inferior, the pilots were inadequately trained, and both were in the air in large numbers. Many successful pilots who had achieved victories in the West were re-assigned to the Eastern Front where they were easily able to improve their scores because of previous experience. As a comparison, in 1941 only seven pilots were awarded the Knight's Cross for combat with the RAF because the standard was 20 victories. In 1942 there were 97 awards for day fighters, seven for night fighters, and six for destroyers despite the fact that 40 victories were required for the first half of the year and 50 for the second half. Pilots who flew combat in the Mediterranean or against England were at a definite disadvantage and only received awards because a small number survived long enough.

Many pilots who were awarded the medal had actually far exceeded the required number of victories by the time the award was presented. As more and more fighter pilots came close to the required number of victories, the High Command feared the medal was again in danger of becoming cheap. In the spring of 1943, the standard had been raised to 75 victories in the East and in November the absolute ceiling of 100 victories was established. As a result in 1943 only 40 fighter, 11 night fighter and two destroyer pilots received the Knight's Cross while fighting against Russia. Once again the requirement was eventually dropped to 75 enemy aircraft destroyed because of the limited number of awards made that year.

Even the lower figure of 75 represented an obstacle because the fighting conditions in the East were rapidly changing. The Russians began to fly better aircraft from 1943 on. Although the Russian pilots were not especially capable in the air, this inferiority was more than made up in the increased number of aircraft they were able to put into the air. At the same time the number of available German pilots decreased as more and more were returned to Germany for home defense. Eventually there were only 300 to 400 fighters assigned to the entire Eastern Front.

As the intensity of the air war in the West increased with the arrival of more and more heavily armed four-engine bombers that were protected by more and more long ranged fighters, Galland came up with the idea of a point system to be used as a new standard for evaluating victories. Some method had to be established to reward the tremendous achievement of shooting down a bomber because it was considered to be the primary danger and thus had to be the preferred target of the fighter pilot. Very few pilots favored attacking bombers over fighter versus fighter combat with its lightening fast reactions, so some inducement had to be offered.

Shooting down a four-engine bomber became worth three points as well as a victory. When a bomber was knocked out of formation, it was worth two points even though it was not destroyed. Experience showed that a crippled bomber falling behind the rest of the formation while smoking badly did not go very far and was eventually brought down, so the pilot who first shot it out of formation was given credit for a victory. Finally, shooting down a crippled bomber counted for one point but no victories. Forty points were required for the Knight's Cross.

From 1943 on it was no longer possible to determine the number of victories credited to an individual by the award of the Knight's Cross because point scores and victory scores were not the same. In addition, when a pilot was transferred from the East where the number of victories required was 75, the victories became points if he shot down RAF or USAAF aircraft. In 1944, 56 Knight's Crosses were awarded to fighter pilots in the East and 39 were awarded in the West to pilots who were flying home defense. At the same time there were scores of 100 plus in the East compared to 20 to 50 in the West. There was little change toward the end of the war, but eventually the destruction of a tank was counted as a full aerial victory which was a clear demonstration of the catastrophic conditions on the Eastern Front.

Other branches of the service felt that fighter pilots were given preference in awards, but this judgment was wrong. Four hundred and thirty-five Knight's Crosses were awarded to day fighter and destroyer pilots with an additional 85 going to night fighter pilots including 14 radio operators. Six hundred and forty awards of the Knight's Cross were made to airmen of the bomber, dive-bomber, and close support units.

Higher classes of the Knight's Cross were awarded for multiples of established norms: Oak Leaves for between 125 to 140 victories in the East and 60 to 70 in the West; Swords to the Oak Leaves for 200 to 250 victories in the East and about 100 in the West. There was often a deviation in the norm when the High Command wished to show individual appreciation.

Another step in the line of medals for combat excellence was the Cup of Honor, a loving cup awarded by Göring accompanied by a sliver framed picture of the *Reich*marshal, himself. This award had precedence in World War I when Baron von Richthofen would purchase a loving cup and have it suitably inscribed each time he gained another confirmed aerial victory. Another distinction was a mention in the *Oberkommando Wermacht* Communiqué, which Adolf Galland won three times. The German Government did not give any special pay for awards or decorations.

Awards were given for the number of combat missions in which the enemy was contacted. Pilots in operational combat units wore Front Flight Wings which came in bronze, silver or gold and branches of the GAF could be determined because fighter pilot wings had an eagle in the middle while pilots in the bomber branch had a bomb and so forth.

The War Service Cross, similar to the USA Bronze Star or Legion of Merit, and the Knight's Cross could also be honorary medals for office workers and administrative officers. Commanding officers or individuals in higher levels of command could be awarded regular combat decorations if they had been exposed at any time to enemy action. For example, Marshal Kesselring was awarded Diamonds for his transport flights across the Mediterranean in the face of heavy enemy opposition when he was in command of the *Luftwaffe* Forces in Africa. General Staff Officers often flew on operational missions just to gain a few medals because they were so necessary for prestige and promotion. Still Hitler sometimes violated his own rules and awarded combat decorations to men who never left their desks, but this did not go over well at all with the front line units even though eventually it became common to award all decorations up to the Knight's Cross for chair born activities. Despite the stiffening criteria for awards late in the war, Galland believed that the fighter arm was always stimulated by the race for decorations, and no great change in policy was needed even if the war had gone on.

All of the Allied Nations had different policies regarding decorations for airmen, and the USAAF adopted consistent policies for both bomber crews and fighter pilots. In bombers five missions resulted in the automatic award of the Air Medal and five Air Medals resulted in the award of the Distinguished Flying Cross for the entire crew. In fighters an Air Medal was awarded for ten combat missions and five Air Medals resulted in the award of the Distinguished Flying Cross. Initially, the Silver Star was awarded for two enemy aircraft destroyed on one mission and the Distinguished Service Cross was awarded for three enemy aircraft destroyed on a single mission. However, as the war progressed these exploits became more or less commonplace, and the practice was stopped. Unusual acts of gallantry were rewarded by both the Distinguished Service Cross and the Silver Star and on very rare occasions (usually fatal) the Congressional Medal of Honor was given. When the award of a medal was repeated, an Oak Leaf Cluster (indicating an additional medal) or a Star (for five additional medals) was presented. Combat pilots were distinguished from others by a rectangular blue patch behind their wings and each pilot was allowed to wear the insignia of his Air Force as a patch on his shoulder.

Just after the war ended a USAAF Colonel who had commanded a Fighter Group was sitting in a Paris sidewalk café when a French Citizen asked him if he would be interested in buying a souvenir of the war. This turned out to be the actual citation Hitler had presented to Werner Mölders who had become one of the *Luftwaffe*'s outstanding fighter pilots with over 100 victories to his credit. The award was the Knight's Cross in Gold with Oak Leaf, Swords and Diamonds, and only seven individuals during the entire war had received this decoration, which was always presented by Hitler. Although the actual medal was missing, the citation consisted of a beautiful parchment bound between wooden covers with a heavy gold cross and wings with a span of about three inches fastened to the front cover.

The Colonel bought the citation for a small sum, saving it in anticipation of a suitable time to return it to the Mölders Family (he had been killed in a He 111 crash while on his way to attend the funeral of General Ernst Udet). In 1960 during a reunion between members of the German Fighter Pilot's Association and a group from the American Fighter Aces Association, the citation was presented to Adolf Galland who eventually returned it to the Mölder's Family. Galland remembered when he had been presented with the same award by Hitler in 1942. At the time Hitler had whispered to him, "Take good care of this, it cost $28,000.00. If the German people ever find out what we pay for these medals they will have my hide."

Regardless of the efforts of the *Luftwaffe* to instill high morale in the forces, there were always minor incidents involving discipline. Punishment for such offenses could be administered by unit commanders or by court martial, but this would vary depending on the severity of the offense such as death for murder and so forth. In addition there were always a number of political offenses such as defeatism and treasonable utterances that were punishable. Before the war, flying discipline in the fighter force was quite relaxed because rashness and daring were encouraged to build up skill and *esprit de corps*. However, after 1935 the accident rate became so high that strong measures had to be taken to counteract the rising tide of carelessness and risk. Initially, the usual punishment for accidents was a short grounding, but it became necessary to administer longer periods of grounding, loss of flight pay, and often transfers into an infantry unit to reduce the number of accidents taking place. Those who were killed due to their own negligence or disobedience were buried without military honors, and their dependents received no pensions. Eventually, this strong policy resulted in suppressing the dash and daring expected of good fighter pilots because both students and instructors began to fly conservatively to avoid risks. Often students who were eventually assigned to fighter schools found the change to realistic fighter flying beyond their capabilities, and high accident rates were the result.

Radio discipline in all units was always poor as a result of limited training, and this problem really became evident whenever German fighter pilots found themselves outnumbered in a battle and felt that they needed help. The GAF tried various measures to control the tendency to talk too much on the air, and among them was the installation of two microphone buttons instead of one, so each pilot would have to make two movements to talk. The GAF also monitored the radio conversations in an effort to punish those who talked too much, but the high turnover rate of pilots made it difficult to determine who had done the talking because the pilots did not have time enough to learn each other's voices over the radio/telephone.

The GAF created a special organization called a *Sturmgruppe* so that people accused of cowardice or other similar offenses could erase these crimes from their records. This organization took special and daring risks against the enemy in combat while flying heavily armed Bf 109s. In the Defense of the *Reich*, so many pilots volunteered for these units because their homes had been destroyed or their families had been killed or injured that only about ten percent were disciplinary cases. There were no orders by Göring or anyone else to shoot down pilots who displayed cowardice in combat and there were no SS men in any of the fighter units. In reality, actual cowardice was very rare and in general there were very few disciplinary difficulties in the fighter arm in spite of the adverse conditions under which this branch of the GAF operated.

CHAPTER SIX

The Machines

The Germans entered the war with what for the time was a formidable fleet consisting of over 4300 aircraft. Altogether there were thirteen day fighter Wings consisting of 771 single seat fighters, 12 equipped with the Messerschmitt Bf 109E and one with the Arado Ar 68. In addition, there were ten Wings of 408 escort fighters and destroyers equipped with the Messerschmitt Bf 110C. There were nine dive-bomber Wings consisting of 336 Junkers Ju 87A's and B's.

The Bf 109 had served its trial under fire in Spain and was acknowledged by intelligence circles of the world as a superior machine. It was a small aircraft with a wing span of only 32 feet 6 inches. Powered by a 1,150 hp liquid cooled engine, it was capable of 354 mph at 12,300 feet and had a range of 621 miles and a service ceiling of 36,000 feet. Equipped with two 20mm cannon, on either wing outside the propeller arc and two 7.7 mm machine guns mounted in the fuselage firing through the propeller, it was able to carry one 500 pound bomb or four 110 pound bombs. As the war progressed various versions of the Bf 109 went into production and eventually this machine was capable of 380 mph at 21,000 feet because additional horsepower had been added.

When the Battle of Britain started the Bf 109 was the best fighter aircraft in the world and became the prototype for international fighter aircraft construction. In addition to the outstanding performance there were several unique design features built into the aircraft. Reloading it with gasoline, oil, coolant, and ammunition took approximately 15 minutes and the engine could be changed in twelve minutes while the servicing was being completed. Because of leading edge slots, which at the time were a great innovation, this little aircraft landed slowly and thus could use quite small airfields. As a slight disadvantage the cockpit was quite small, but larger pilots found that it was possible to remove the seat and sit on the floor when flying this machine.

The first prototype Bf 110A, then called an escort fighter or Destroyer, flew for the first time in May 1936, and quantity production of the Bf 110C that was equipped with two 1,000 hp liquid cooled engines was ordered in 1938. This aircraft was of medium size with a wingspan of 53 feet 5 inches, and a maximum weight of 16,500 pounds. Capable of a maximum speed of 350 mph at 23,000 feet the Bf 110 exceeded all *Luftwaffe* expectations as an escort fighter and Destroyer during the war in Spain, the campaign in Poland and finally during the sweep through the Low Countries and France. Since it was equipped with 5 machine guns and 2 x 20mm cannons, the Bf 110 proved especially effective during the early days as an attack fighter and the later installation of bomb and rocket racks gave it more than adequate dive bombing ability. Characteristically, the *Luftwaffe* continually upgraded the performance of the Bf 110 by adding more powerful engines and heavier armament. Still during the Battle of Britain Bf 110 units received terrible punishment from the British Spitfire and Hurricane fighter pilots. It eventually became relegated to the role of Destroyer only when Allied fighter aircraft were not expected in the combat areas. Altogether 5,762 Bf 110s were built in various versions, but the *Luftwaffe* dream of a multi purpose twin-engine fighter aircraft was never quite realized.

The Kondor Legion in Spain had been quite successful in using the Ju 87 Stuka in dive bombing missions. Although this aircraft was relatively slow, even for that period, the *Luftwaffe* High Command was impressed with its ability, especially after it achieved even greater successes during the blitzkrieg of Poland, the Low Countries and France. However, during these campaigns the Germans had complete air superiority so it was difficult for enemy fighters to penetrate the escort cover to bring down the dive bombing Stuka. This was a large single engine aircraft with a wing span of 45 feet 4 inches and weighing 14,300 lbs at maximum, it was equipped with two machine guns mounted in the wings and it could carry one 550 pound bomb mounted on a sling underneath the center of the fuselage. Because of a fixed undercarriage, it was very slow, capable of flying at maximum speed of only 255 mph at 15,000 feet. During the Battle of Britain it became so vulnerable to enemy attack that it was withdrawn from combat, although it was used on the Eastern Front against Russia right up to the end of the war.

The Focke-Wulf Fw 190A was one of the outstanding single-engine fighters to see combat during World War II. Designed by the famous German Professor Kurt Tank, the Fw 190 first appeared over the English Channel during the summer of 1941, immediately showing a marked superiority over the British Spitfire Mark V. The Fw 190 was considered to be small with a wing span of only 34 feet 6 inches. With a maximum weight of 9,200 pounds and a range of 530 miles, it had a speed of 395 mph at 17,000 feet. This machine could carry several combinations of machine guns and cannon. The most popular configuration was 4x20mm cannon and one 1,100 lb bomb. Altogether 13,367 fighters and 6,634 fighter-bomber versions were produced and the Germans were able to make constant improvements that always resulted in increased performance. The Fw 190 had several outstanding flight characteristics. It was very light on the ailerons and had a rapid rate of roll. It would accelerate rapidly in a dive, but its light-weight prevented it from reaching near sonic diving speeds. In a climb it would gain altitude rapidly but at a relatively slow forward speed. It was easy to fly and its wide spread landing gear made it easy to land. It was well armored and its radial engine was not only reliable but also provided protection for the pilot when he was making attacks on heavy bombers that were firing back. Because it could absorb great punishment and did have high performance most German fighter pilots felt that the Fw 190 was so much better than the Bf 109 that production of the Messerschmitt should have been discontinued in order to increase production on the Focke-Wulf.

The Fw 190D modification was made by installing a liquid cooled in line 12 cylinder engine in place of the radial engine of the original design. Outward appearances were changed slightly because the aircraft had a longer nose, but it still had a radial engine appearance because the coolant radiator was cylindrical and was mounted directly behind the propeller. The Fw 190D was slightly heavier than earlier versions, but it had a maximum speed of 426 mph at 21,500 feet with a range of 550 miles. This aircraft was first flown in 1941 but did not begin combat operations until the winter of 1943-1944.

Long before the Russians and the Allies broke through the Ober and Rhine lines respectively, the Germans were still presuming that they had a chance of winning the war. In early 1945, the *Luftwaffe* planners were still devising methods for up-grading the caliber and quantity of fighters to be used in turning back the Allied Air Armadas and these plans were all based on the front lines stabilizing as they were at the time. In reality, the Allied thrusts from both East and West made the air war impossible for the Germans and finally resulted in the effective dissolution of the *Luftwaffe* by the end of April that year. Until that time, however, the fighter arm was still vigorously attempting to continue the defensive war in the air and great attention was directed toward improving the equipment.

The technical effort was always directed toward the development of high altitude fighters with very long range. Professor Kurt Tank was given permission to use the Ta prefix on all aircraft he designed and the Ta 152 which was similar to the Fw 190 in appearance was the most promising piston engine fighter to result from his efforts. This was a heavier aircraft weighing 12,125 pounds with a wing span of 47 feet 7 inches. It was powered with a 1,880 hp in line liquid cooled engine that gave it a speed of 469 mph at 40,000 feet. Equipped with one 30mm cannon and two 20mm cannon and steel wings, the aircraft was intended to be the perfect *Sturm* fighter designed specifically to bring down four-engine heavy bombers and its range of 750 miles gave it the capability for repeated strikes against enemy formations. Series production was started very late so there was only one Group of Ta 152's in operation at the end of the war.

The Germans planned to cancel production of both the Fw 190 and the Bf 109 in order to increase production of more highly developed aircraft with higher performance and increased striking power. The newer aircraft were to be equipped with machine guns of heavier caliber, a more rapid rate of fire, a range of over 800 meters, and superior ballistics. Rockets were to eventually replace cannon for use against bombers and the Germans were at work developing a seeking head. They had designed a gyroscopic gun sight that was to become standard equipment and were developing a radar ranging device for the new sight. Special high altitude cabins with adequate heating and de-icing and high altitude parachutes equipped with a supply of oxygen and a barometric release had been perfected for high altitude aircraft. Since it had been found that gasoline was carried most efficiently in external fuel tanks when they were located over the wing roots either flared in or mounted directly on top of the wings, production was under way on these new types.

The Germans had developed a new radio navigation system that used various ground stations. By a simple stop-click method of tuning in these stations the pilot would have a grid map display which would have the coordinates of his position on a sliding scale, and thus navigation would have been reduced to a minimum of pilot effort.

Almost all these innovations had application on the next series of fighters to see combat which were typified by the Do 335. This aircraft which was to be the ultimate Destroyer was designed to destroy heavy bombers at long ranges and yet would have the capability of outrunning the Allied fighter escort. This was a most unusual design with an in-line liquid cooled engine in both front and rear. The aircraft first flew in the fall of 1943, and went into series production in 1944, but the Germans had already lost almost two years of usefulness because they did not make the decision to produce the aircraft even though the designs were completed much, much earlier. The machine was quite large with a wing-span of 45 feet four inches it weighed 26,000 pounds and had a maximum speed of 417 mph at 26,000 feet. Each engine produced 1,900 hp, and the aircraft had a range of 1,300 miles, which was excellent for the time. It could deliver a bomb load of 1,100 pounds and was equipped with two 20mm and one 30mm cannon. Although the machine was weird and ungainly in appearance, it was an outstanding fighter (but only 35 production craft had been completed by the end of the war).

The revolutionary advent of jet propulsion gave the Germans the potential for turning back the Allied Air Armadas, but Hitler prevented the Fighter Forces from capitalizing on this innovation until it was too late to alter the course of the air war. Of all of the rocket and jet propelled aircraft the Germans had either produced or had in the initial stages of development, the Me 262 was the most promising. This machine was fairly small for a twin-engine fighter weighing only 14,000 pounds. With a wing span of 41 feet it was able to climb to 26,000 feet in 11 minutes, and had a maximum speed at 22,960 feet of 525 mph. This was at least 100 mph faster than contemporary piston engine fighters at that time.

This aircraft had four 30mm cannon in the nose, and two external bomb racks under the fuselage capable of carrying 500 kg bombs. There were several radical innovations built into the aircraft including a small two-cycle gasoline engine in each of the jet engine nacelles to enable engine starts without an external power supply.

The Me 262 was first flown on May 22, 1943, and in early test flights achieved the speed of 520 mph in horizontal flight. This sensational jump in technology was the answer to the German fighter pilot's dream, and was especially attractive to the High Command because it used inferior fuel and high octane gasoline was becoming increasingly difficult to supply. Professor Messerschmitt had recommended that series production be initiated with a minimum quantity of 100 aircraft. Hitler was determined to develop the He 177 four-engine heavy bomber even though it meant a delay in production of the jet fighter so he would not authorize mass production of the Me 262 although limited flight-testing was allowed to continue. Approximately 18 months of production of the Me 262 were lost because the High Command did not become interested and sanction full mass production with top priority until the end of 1943.

As hints of the jet propelled Me 262 gradually filtered out of Germany to the Allied intelligence organizations there was great consternation. Fighter pilots and bomber crews were cautioned to be on the look out for strange types of fighters because aerial photographs had revealed odd looking aircraft parked on various airfields known to be used for flight test research. This consternation however, was nothing compared to what was happening in Germany because of Hitler's intransigence.

Albert Speer in his book, *Inside The Third Reich,* recalled the situation this way:

> "As early as 1941, while I was still an architect, I had paid a visit to the Heinkel aircraft plant at Rostock and heard the deafening noise of one of the first jet engines on a testing stand. The designer, Professor Ernst Heinkel was urging that this revolutionary advance be applied to aircraft construction. During the armaments congress at the Air Force test site in Rechlin (September 1943) Milch, then Armaments Chief of the Air Force, silently handed me a telegram that had just been brought to him. It contained an order from Hitler to halt preparations for large scale production of the Me 262. We decided to

circumvent this order. But still the work could not be continued on the priority basis it should have had.

"Some three months later, on January 7,1944, Milch and I were urgently summoned to headquarters. Hitler had changed his mind and this on the basis of an excerpt from the British press on the success of British experiments with jet planes. He was now impatient to have as many aircraft of this type as we could make in the shortest possible time. In the meantime, Hitler had let everything lapse, we could promise to deliver no more than sixty planes a month from July 1944 on. From January 1945 on, however, we would be able to produce two hundred and ten aircraft a month.

"In the course of this conference Hitler indicated that he planned to use the plane, which was built as a fighter, as a fast bomber. The Air Force specialists were dismayed, but imagined that their sensible arguments would prevail. What happened was just the opposite. Hitler obstinately ordered all weapons on board to be removed so that the aircraft would carry a greater weight of bombs. Jet planes did not have to defend themselves, he maintained, since with their superior speed they would not be attacked by enemy fighters.

"The effect of these tiny bombers, which could carry a load of little more than a thousand pounds of bombs and had only a primitive bombsight was ridiculously insignificant. As fighter planes, on the other hand, each one of the jet aircraft would have been able, because of its superior performance, to shoot down several of the four-motored American bombers which in raid after raid were dropping thousands of tons of bombs on German cities."

Speer went on to say:

"It was true, of course, that the planes in question existed so far only in a few prototypes. Nevertheless, Hitler's order necessarily influenced long ranged planning, for the General Staff had been counting on this new type of fighter to bring about a decisive turning point in the air war. Desperate as we were over this aspect of the war, every one who could claim any knowledge of the subject at all put in a word and tried to change Hitler's mind. Jodl, Guderian, Model, Sepp Dietrich, and of course the leading Generals of the Air Force persistently took issue with Hitler's layman opinion. But they only brought his anger down on their heads since he took all this as an attack on his military expertise and technical intelligence. In the autumn of 1944 he finally and characteristically brushed aside the whole controversy by flatly forbidding any further discussion of the subject."

While the controversy was raging over the Me 262, the German Air Ministry in September 1944 issued a specification for a "Peoples Fighter" or *Volksjager* and the specifications for this machine included that it had to be constructed with non-strategic materials in the shortest possible time. Based on maximum simplicity, the He 162 with a jet engine outfitted on top of the fuselage was completed in December 1944 as a result. The fuselage was of all metal construction with a wooden nose cap, gun bay doors, and landing gear doors. Wings, movable surfaces, and twin rudders were also made of wood. This little aircraft had a wingspan of 23 feet 8 inches and had a maximum weight of only 6,000 pounds. It was capable of 500 mph at 20,000 feet and had a range of 400 miles. It could be equipped with either two 30mm or two 20mm cannon. Altogether 120 aircraft were completed by the end of the war, but fighter pilots felt that it never lived up to its promise. In their views the aircraft had one thing in its favor, it could never have been used as a fast bomber.

Another fighter that could never have been converted to any sort of bomber was the rocket propelled Me 163, which when introduced in combat in 1944, was a tremendous surprise to Allied heavy bomber crews. This tiny, tailless aircraft was propelled by a bi-fuel, liquid rocket engine that gave it the ability to climb to 30,000 feet in 2.6 minutes. The aircraft was of all wooden construction with a pronounced wing sweep back and a span of only 30 feet 7 inches. It had a maximum weight of only 9,500 pounds. The main wheels of the aircraft were jettisoned on take off and in landing the pilot extended a short skid that made each touch down almost an emergency.

The aircraft was fueled with 210 gallons of hydrogen peroxide and 130 gallons of hydrazine solution in methanol, an extremely volatile combination. The fuel tanks were pressurized so the fuel would be forced into the combustion chamber and the pilots had instructions to bail out regardless of location if the pressure fell below a certain point in either tank. Considered to be extremely dangerous to fly by all pilots, the aircraft was highly effective in combat against heavy bombers. Equipped with two 30mm cannon it could carry various combinations of rockets under the wings.

As spectacular as this aircraft was, it was shrouded by other developments that caught Hitler's fancy. The rocket propelled Natter was to all intents and purposes a piloted missile that was launched vertically to attack bomber formations in a matter of a few minutes. After firing twenty-four rockets the pilot was expected to bail out and descend safely by parachute. On the first flight of this device when it became airborne it proved to be unstable and the pilot was killed when the canopy broke his neck as he released it to bail out.

V-1 and V-2 rockets were given top priority in production at the expense of manned fighter aircraft even though the total planned production would enable the Germans to deliver such a small amount of explosives against England that it would be only a drop in the bucket when compared to the tonnage being dropped by the Allied Air Armadas at the time. The designers even constructed a piloted version of the V-1 Buzz Bomb that was flown by a famous woman test pilot. The problem with this approach was that the pilot would have either been killed when the bomb struck its target or captured when he bailed out in the target area.

Albert Speer described the situation that confronted the Fighter Forces in the latter part of 1944 as follows:

> "Fighter Commander Adolf Galland and I had calculated that on the average one German fighter plane would be lost over Germany in order to shoot down a bomber, but that the expenditure of material on both sides would be in proportion of one to two and the attrition of pilots one to two. Moreover, since half of our downed pilots would parachute safely to the ground, while enemy crews would be taken prisoner on German soil, the advantage was surely on our side, even giving the enemy superiority in men, materials, and training potential.
>
> "Around August 10th Galland, in extreme agitation, asked me to fly with him to headquarters at once. In one of his arbitrary decisions Hitler had issued new orders: The *Reich* air fleet whose outfitting with two thousand planes (in preparation for a giant blow against

the Allied Forces) was nearing completion, was suddenly shifted to the Western Front. There, experience had long since shown us, it would be wiped out within a short time.

"Hitler, of course, guessed why we were visiting him. He knew he had broken the promise he gave me in July to have the hydrogenation plants protected by fighter planes. But he forestalled a quarrel at the situation conference and agreed to receive us alone afterwards. I began by cautiously expressing doubts of the usefulness of his order and mastered my strong feelings by explaining as calmly as possible the catastrophic situation in armaments production. I cited figures and sketched the consequences that would follow from continued bombings. That alone made Hitler nervous and angry. Although he listened in silence, I could see by his expression, by the lively fluttering of his hands, the way he chewed his fingernails that he was growing increasingly tense. When I finished, thinking that I had amply proved that every available plane in the *Reich* should be employed to combat bombers, Hitler was no longer in control of himself. His face had flushed deep red and his eyes had turned lifeless and fixed. Then he roared out at the top of his lungs: "Operative measures are my concern! Kindly concern yourself with your armaments! This is none of your business." Possibly he might have been more receptive had I talked to him privately. The presence of Galland made him incapable of understanding or flexibility. Abruptly he terminated the conference, cutting off all further argument. "I have no further time for you." Galland and I returned to my barracks office.

"The next day we were on the point of flying back to Berlin, our mission a failure, when Schaub informed us that we were to report to Hitler again. This time Hitler's rage was even more violent; he spoke faster and faster, stumbling over his own words: "I want no-more planes produced at all. The fighter arm is to be dissolved. Stop aircraft production! Stop it at once, understand? You're always complaining about the shortage of skilled workers, aren't you? Put them into flak production at once. Let all the workers produce anti-aircraft guns. Use all the material for that too! Now, that's an order. Send Saur to headquarters immediately. A program for flak production must be set up. Tell Saur that too. A program five times what we have now. We'll shift hundreds of thousands of workers into flak production.

Every day I read in the foreign press reports of how dangerous flak is. They still have some respect for that, but not for our fighters." Galland started to reply that the fighters would shoot down far more planes if they could be committed inside Germany, but he did not get beyond the first words. Again we were abruptly dismissed, actually thrown out."

Finally, in his manuscript Speer noted:

"When on March 22, 1945, Hitler invited me to one of his armaments conferences, I again had Saur represent me. From his notes it was clear that he and Hitler had frivolously ignored the realities. The minutes also recorded an order of Hitler's that five new variants of existing types of tanks were to be demonstrated to him within a few weeks. In addition, he wanted to investigate the effect of Greek fire, known since classical antiquity, and he wished to have our jet fighter-bomber, the Me 262, re-armed as quickly as possible as a fighter plane. In ordering this last action, he was tacitly conceding the error he had made a year and one half before when he had persistently refused the advice of all the experts."

It was apparent from that point on that Hitler would frantically attempt to create new wonder weapons from existing equipment, so the German scientific community began to furiously improve whatever they could. Plans were under way to further develop the Me 262 in order to increase range and performance with the addition of external fuel tanks and a built-in Walther rocket engine that was to be used to increase the climbing speed. The Germans intended to add to the amount of armor protection for the pilot and engines, and more and heavier armament was to be added to increase the capability for attacking heavy bombers. Since the He 162 was already at the limit of its capability, the Germans only considered adding a rocket engine to increase climb performance, but the Me 163 was to be replaced by an advanced version, the Me 263, which would have double the endurance and much heavier armament. Rockets were to be added in the wings of the Me 262 in such a way that they could be fired either vertically up or down. A whole new series of piloted rockets such as the Natter were to be developed for the Fighter Arm. The fighter arm was selected because pilots from any other branch of the service would have required special fighter training in order to fly them.

Since the fighter forces were fully committed to the defensive at the time, each Group was to be held at a maximum strength of about 70 aircraft of which about 50 could be expected to be serviceable at any one time. This limit was established because it had been found to be the maximum number that could start and assemble in a reasonable length of time. It was necessary to have large Groups so that a greater number of fighter aircraft could be flown from the limited number of operational airfields within Germany. Operations had to be conducted in group strength instead of the very large *Gefechtsverband*s of wing size because it was too difficult to assemble these larger units in time to make attacks on attacking bomber formations. It was planned that each Group would fly within sight of each other while maintaining radio contact so each could support the other. The old type of strict Division control over the fighters was to be abandoned, and each Group Commander was to have tactical freedom about how and when he attacked the bomber stream.

Fighter unit mobility would have been no longer necessary once the front lines became stabilized because of the limited geography that was available in Germany. The fighter forces were to be divided into light and heavy groups depending upon the mission of attacking enemy fighter escort or the heavy bomber formations. It was anticipated that all units would be used from time to time to support the Army at the front lines. The heavy Groups were to be trained to fire rockets and drop bombs while the light Groups would be required to strafe and fight off enemy fighters over the battle area. The *Luftwaffe* was concerned that the Allied heavy bombers would eventually begin to attack at a bombing altitude of about 5000 feet thus making all the existing high altitude German fighters ineffective, so the Ta 152 production was to be increased to forestall this eventuality. For the future, the *Luftwaffe* planned to convert almost the entire conventional fighter force to the Ta 152 for lower altitude work and the Bf 109H would be used for high altitude. It was intended that a small force of single engine night fighters would be available in case the defensive air intercept radar was jammed so at least these aircraft could put up some sort of defense. Since almost all of the twin-engine fighter units had been dissolved or converted to single-engine aircraft in early 1944, it was planned to re-equip them with the Do 335s. The *Luftwaffe* still used older twin-engine fighters to cover the U-boats of the Navy as they approached land.

The Germans already had found the use of the Me 262 and the Me 163 required innovations in fighter organization and control. Each Group was to have three Squadrons of twelve aircraft each, with a total of 40 aircraft including the Group Headquarters Flight. It was anticipated that about 25 aircraft would be serviceable at any one time, so this size would not be too large for the normal German airfields that were available at the time. Operations had revealed that each flight should consist of three aircraft instead of four. Wings were to consist of three groups with their own fighter ground control capability because larger units would have been unwieldy in the air since the employment of jets placed a greater demand on the controllers. It was also discovered quite early that the great speed of these new fighters made it necessary to give precise information on the location of enemy forces and exact vectoring was required to make an intercept. The whole problem of utilizing the Me 262 effectively had been complicated by Hitler's various orders that it was to be used only as a fast light bomber. The situation was even further complicated by Göring who further implemented Hitler's instructions by giving most of the aircraft to converted bomber Wings in the hopes that the pilots and ground crews would be able to conduct fighter bomber type operations in time to effect the outcome of the ground war. Galland hoped to use the vastly superior Me 262 against Allied fighter escort thus tying up the enemy by repeatedly diving and climbing to regain favorable positions after once attacking with this approach. GAF conventional fighters would have been able to attack the bomber formations relatively unmolested as they had been trained to do and as the aircraft they flew had been designed for.

Actually, this plan was never put into operation because by the time the Me 262 units were ready for operations the GAF conventional fighter forces had almost ceased to exist and the Me 262's had to attack the bombers because nothing else was capable of doing so. By early 1945, the two existing Me 262 Wings enjoyed considerable success because they were able to disregard the Allied fighters while making attacks on the bomber formations. Previously the ratio of victories to losses in conventional fighters had been.1 to 5, but this ratio was reversed with the Me 262 and the units suffered only one loss for every five victories.

Operational use of the He 162 *Volksjager* (Peoples Fighter) presented even more very special problems since the aircraft did not perform up to specifications. The aircraft was never satisfactory although initially the Heinkel Company had promised it would have performance equal to the Me 262. The aircraft went directly into production from the blueprint stage without the usual flight-testing and although this was a marvelous feat of production, performance suffered because the additional necessary development changes were not discovered in the experimental stages. In Galland's opinion the He 162 was not even ready for combat at the end of the war. Since this aircraft only had about 20 minutes total endurance, ground operations were extremely critical. It was necessary to program landings and take-off very skillfully to avoid Allied fighter escort because the aircraft was very vulnerable with flaps down. He 162s were to be employed as regional fighters defending certain geographical areas, and it would have been necessary to have ground to air controllers and their organizations within the wing structure of the He 162 units. Although organized like the Me 262 Wings, it would have been impossible to have these two types of aircraft operating in the same air space together because of their dissimilar performance.

At one time it was proposed to operate both at the same time, but the idea was given up because only the Me 262s would have had radios that were necessary for air ground communications. The rocket propelled Me 163 was even worse because it had a radius of action of only about 35 miles and even this much range was difficult to achieve because there was so little fuel on board. About 50 aircraft were produced per month, but this was an adequate number because the limited engagements with the enemy resulted in very few losses. The three Groups that were equipped with the Me 163 were organized like the me 262 Groups with three Squadrons of 12 aircraft each, but every landing with the me 163 was considered an emergency so only one Group was located on each airfield. Because of their limited range, these aircraft operated singularly instead of in formation, although they tried to attack the enemy bombers in concentration whenever possible. Fighter control with this aircraft was even more difficult than with the 262's because each second in the air was important and each individual aircraft had to be controlled separately. Under ground control the Me 163 would climb at an angle of attack of about 50 to an altitude of about 3,000 feet above the bombers than shut off power to estimate the situation. The pilot then made his attack at gliding speed, turning on power only to dive away. Although dangerous to operate from the standpoint of the pilot, this was a desirable aircraft from a total resources standpoint since the fuel it used was not required from the supply used by other types. In addition, it started from tracks with rocket assist, and could have operated from the Autobahn. Developments of newer versions like the Me 263 had about three times the range and more firepower than the earlier versions.

Single-engine fighter units often used poorly equipped grass airfields without hangers or runways, and aircraft were often dispersed as much as three miles away from the airfields because of the threat posed by Allied aircraft attacks. Early in the war when the *Luftwaffe* proposed construction of newer and larger airfields, they met strong opposition by the lumber and farming interests, but even still in early 1944 plans were made for the expansion or new construction of about 150 airfields inside Germany. Some were to be built on old airfields, and some on the Autobahn. Since pilots of conventional aircraft did not like runways, the Autobahn was to be used for jet operations. Eventually, the shortage of materials prevented most of the new construction.

Hitler had always advocated the construction of large circular bunkers to protect aircraft near airfields, but Galland objected on the grounds that a carpet of bombs laid over the bunkers would prevent undamaged aircraft from taxiing out. However, some bunkers were actually constructed, but it was found that they were better utilized for repair shops than for parking aircraft. Still, most units depended on dispersal and camouflage for protection. Because they had difficulty in taxiing, jet aircraft needed special concrete aprons at the end of the runways where they could be lined up for fast take off. Although it was best to have a motorized tug available for each aircraft, many units only had one for three because ground support equipment was in very short supply. When conventional fighter units were increased in size in late 1944, this shortage became even more pronounced. Despite all efforts to build new airfields and improve old ones, there were never enough because fields that were built or improved were usually near the front and were over-run by the enemy. The Germans depended upon light flak for protection from low level attacks, and each airfield had its own flak company under the *Luftgaue*. Small caliber guns were used, many coming from the .50 caliber weapons retrieved from downed American bombers. Most airfields had over 200 anti-aircraft guns, but the jet airfields had even more because jets were slow in taking off and landing and required greater protection. Galland considered flak protection to have been very effective.

Conventional fighter training which had been drastically curtailed during the war by fuel shortages was very inadequate. If all other branches of the *Luftwaffe* except day and night fighters had canceled flying training, some increase in the total number of fighter pilots trained would have been possible, but the High Command would never agree to this course of action. Hitler wanted bombers, reconnaissance, and so forth and no one dared to try to change his mind. Galland wanted to allocate new pilots directly to the Me 262 units where they would be trained by actually going out on combat operations instead of wasting time and fuel in the operational training units before joining a combat organization. Eventually, Me 262s would have to be assigned to operational training units when production would have permitted doing so and ultimately they would have filtered down to the fighter flying schools, but of course this all would have depended upon loss rates and production quantities. Only one Wing was able to carry out this concept. Only the Bomber wings were given the Me 262 first because of Hitler's wishes. Not much training was ever done on the Me 262s because of the confusing instructions that Hitler gave out. Besides, experienced pilots could cope with the aircraft without much transition flying, and all of the aircraft were needed immediately to combat the enemy.

Luftwaffe Headquarters first proposed that the He 162 pilots would be trained entirely in gliders, but Galland killed this idea for obvious reasons. Instead, a plan was approved which would give He 162 pilots training in gliders built just like the actual powered aircraft prior to training with powered versions. Pilots would also be given training in the Bf 109 and the Fw 190 as transition aircraft, but fuel shortages forced cancellation of this concept after a short while. At one time it was considered that the *Gauleiter* Political Governors were to control combat operations of the He 162 because it was the People's Fighter, but this crazy idea was stopped just in time before it could become a disaster. For training on the Me 163, pilots went to the usual preliminary flying training and then onto regular flying schools where they received everything but formation flying. They first encountered the Me 163 in Operational Training Units where they made unloaded, towed flights, loaded towed flights, half loaded powered flights, and finally five fully loaded powered flights before going into operational units. More flights were not possible because of the shortage of C-Stoff fuel made the whole program very limited in scope. The entire operation was complicated even more because the me 163 required special fuel handling equipment and great quantities of clean running water not available at ordinary airfields.

The Germans had interesting opinions regarding the capabilities of Allied aircraft, but their mastery of jet propulsion had a lot of influence on their thinking. It was hard for them to give a good opinion of any piston engine aircraft after flying or even working with jets, so they were not laudatory about any Allied machine. The Germans had large numbers of captured or downed Allied aircraft in their possession, and they even used fairly large formations of American B-17s to test combat tactics. Most of the combat leaders had flown captured fighters, so performance characteristics were quite well known. In addition the Allies had more or less stabilized on specific types in order to achieve high production rates so there were relatively few innovations or surprises. In the course of the war the British clipped wings on the Spitfire to achieve desirable performance improvements and they continually increased the horsepower and range by addition of larger engines with better fuel consumption. The Americans made innovations such as water injection and paddle bladed propellers to increase performance and various combinations of internal and external fuel tanks were designed to extend range. They did not, however, achieve a quantum jump as the Germans did by sending jet-propelled aircraft into combat.

The Germans considered the Hurricane to be a rugged aircraft, but felt it was much too slow for a modern fighter. During the Battle of Britain, it was equipped with 12 machine guns, so they felt that it was maneuverable and effective against their bombers. The aircraft was even more effective when modified to carry four 20mm cannon and German Intelligence information revealed that it had destroyed as many aircraft (mostly bombers) as the Spitfires. It performed well in the role of Destroyer when used mainly against bombers while being covered and supported by Spitfires.

The Germans considered the British Typhoon to be an exceptionally fast aircraft able to outrun both the Bf 109 and the Fw 190 in level flight.

It had excellent armament for ground strafing, but was not maneuverable enough to dog fight with either the Bf 109 or the Fw 190. The American Lockheed P-38 was also considered to be very fast, with a good rate of climb below 20,000 feet. However, visibility to the rear, below, or over the engines was very poor, it lacked maneuverability, and was quite vulnerable to enemy fire. Although the combination of four machine guns and one cannon made it effective in strafing attacks and it could out-run the Bf 109 and Fw 190, German fighter pilots always preferred to attack this type in preference to other Allied escort fighters.

In Africa everyone thought the Airacobra, P-39 to be inferior even early in the Allied war. It had poor maneuverability, speed, climb and diving performance and was one of the easiest fighters to shoot down. The same opinion held true for the P-40 Warhawk which was also inferior as a modern fighter. The P-40 was slow, could not climb or dive and was considered to be too lightly armed because it only had four 50-caliber machine-guns. However, the P-40 could out turn both the Bf 109 and the Fw 190 in a dogfight below 12,000 feet.

The Germans felt that the P-51 Mustang was the best American fighter because it had long range, good climb and dive characteristics, good maneuverability and adequate firepower. However, it was valuable to cannon fire and would break up in flight during violent dives and maneuvers. This was caused in part by the installation of an aft fuselage fuel tank that caused a slight tail heavy condition when full. The Germans believed the P-47 Thunderbolt to be just an adequate fighter aircraft which was exceptionally fast in a dive although it could be out distanced initially by the Bf 109. Their experience indicated that it could absorb many cannon hits and still fly home, so this made it desirable as a ground support fighter. In his book, *The First and The Last,* Adolf Galland had the following comments on the British Mosquito which was used by the RAF for the same type of missions the *Luftwaffe* employed the Destroyers:

"A special chapter was the fight against the Mosquito. England had developed an all purpose aircraft with an extraordinary performance whose action over Germany caused a lot of trouble. The twin-engine De Havilland had a speed that none of our fighter planes could approach. By day it flew on reconnaissance flights at high altitude, but it also performed bombing missions. It had a very precise bombsight called "Oboe." It was successful, at little cost, in nuisance raids at night. Until we were able to send up the Me 262 jet fighter planes, we were practically powerless against the Mosquitoes. Like their namesake, they became a plague to our Command and our population. Our fighters could only catch up with them when we dived on them from a much greater height during an attack, temporarily achieving higher speed. But as the Mosquitoes already flew at a great height, this maneuver could only be performed when the approach of the aircraft was discovered early enough and it could be passed on from one radar station to another. Here were the difficulties: First, our radar network was by no means without gaps, and second, the Mosquito was of wooden construction, so this little "bird" only gave a very faint signal in our sites. These were the facts that one simply had to accept for the time being. Anyhow, with this aircraft alone the German war industry could not be hit decisively. There was no danger that we might lose the war on account of the Mosquito. It was for quite different reasons that Göring went mad about our inability to stop these raids. In daytime they flew without loses and went where ever their mission took them. At night they chased the population out of their beds. The latter who were justifiably annoyed at this, started to grumble, "The Fat One can't even cope with a few silly mosquitoes."

Ignoring me, Göring recalled two experienced group leaders from the east and ordered them to clear up this daily nuisance in one way or another. Two strengthened flights were formed especially for this purpose, bombastically christened 25th and 50th Fighter Wings. The aircraft were "souped up" by all sorts of tricks. Special methods of attack were worked out. Without avail! As far as I know neither of these units ever shot down a Mosquito! They were dissolved in autumn, 1943 and I was able to use the aircraft in general Defense of the *Reich*."

There was no doubt on both sides that the advent of the jet propelled fighter and the advantage it gave to the *Luftwaffe* could easily have turned the tide of the air battles over Europe. The German industrial machine had made tremendous engineering strides in designing a large number of excellent jet fighters and bombers, all of which came close to large series production. Still, conflicting directives from Hitler and the High Command kept the aircraft that were put into operational use from being utilized in the best way. In spite of help from Albert Speer, the industry was not allowed to concentrate on jet fighter production alone, since Hitler could never bring himself to realize that total concentration on air defense was the only thing that could save Germany.

CHAPTER SEVEN

The Destroyers

During the years 1935 and 1936, the German Air Force made the decision to create a twin-engine fighter force that was to be called the *Zerstörer* Arm or more literally, the Destroyer Arm. These aircraft were to be used to escort bombers, for strategic fighter missions beyond the penetrating range of single-engine fighter for ground attacks, fast bomber missions and day fighter escort missions. Early in 1939 twin-engine aircraft were first used for fast bomber missions against England, but this tactic was ultimately determined to be a mistake because of extremely heavy losses. Since speed, climbing ability, maximum altitude and maneuverability determined whether or not these large machines could out fight small singled fighter aircraft, the addition of rearward armament, a two man crew, blind flying equipment and great range put them at a disadvantage when ever the smaller aircraft were engaged in combat. Only when the jet powered Me 262 or the Dornier 335 went into operation did the *Luftwaffe* have *Zerstörer* aircraft capable of holding their own with existing single-engine enemy fighter aircraft.

Very early on *Luftwaffe* made the absolute decision that the Destroyer would be the long range fighter, so any development that would have transformed existing single-engine types into long range fighters like the American Mustang was not even considered. Because there were such long lead times required for any kind of new development, the *Luftwaffe* never did have a fighter with high performance and long endurance so necessary for both air defense and strategic operations. Inadequate twin-engine fighter aircraft were dissipated into units which conducted all sorts of missions with little or no over all effect on the outcome of the air war.

Zerstörergeschwader, or Destroyer Wings, each had two or three Groups and each Group had three Squadrons plus a Staff Company. With the exception of the fact that each Squadron had 12 aircraft assigned, this organization was somewhat like a single-engine fighter Wing, but it depended on airfield servicing companies just as the bomber and Stuka units did.

Throughout the Polish Campaign only one Destroyer unit was actually in action and this unit scored a limited number of aerial victories with quite small losses because there were no worthy opponents. It did, however, have excellent success with low level attacks against ground targets. When the Polish Campaign was over, this unit was transferred to Jever near Wilhelmshaven and directed to protect coastal areas by pursuing enemy aircraft out over the ocean as far as possible. The unit was also used to make attacks on ground targets in Norway in 1939 and to participate in aerial warfare over the North Sea Coast. During this period the Destroyers were able to score about the same number of aerial victories as the single-engine fighter forces did in the same area. These successes convinced Göring and the *Luftwaffe* High Command that this type of aircraft had great promise, so operational planning provided that greater numbers of Destroyer aircraft would be produced by German Industry. To keep up with an increased demand for twin-engine pilots, in January 1940. Göring personally recruited pilots from single-engine fighter units for the *Zerstörer* arm by advocating that these were to be elite units.

With the invasion and subsequent capture of Norway and Denmark, the *Luftwaffe* increased the twin-engine fighter force in those areas by adding an additional Wing. When the first British carrier aircraft appeared over Norway, one Squadron of Bf 110s was equipped with 900 liter external fuel tanks in order to give them the capability to escort German bomber formations en route from Narvik to Trondheim. During this period the Destroyers scored several victories over carrier based British aircraft because most of these were obsolete wood and fabric machines which were easily shot down by the more modern twin-engine aircraft with much higher performance.

In anticipation of the Campaign in the West, the *Luftwaffe* ordered an increase in production of the Bf 110 in order to form new units and eventually there were three *Zerstörer* Wings available for combat against the Allies. In the first ten days of operations against the enemy all these units scored considerable success by shooting down a large number of Belgian and Dutch fighters in aerial combat. They also proved to be especially effective in low-level attacks against airfields, anti-aircraft positions, and troop columns. However, the French pilots were different, and, after a few moments of uncertainty, Morane Fighters attacked the *Zerstörer* formations only to discover that these aircraft could be shot down with surprising ease, thus greatly increasing the number of losses. When the campaign ended abruptly at Dunkirk, two of the Destroyer Wings were designated to become the Night Fighter Arm of the *Luftwaffe* in anticipation of an assault on England.

When the Battle of Britain finally began, several Destroyer Wings were deployed to France with their Groups located in the area of Laval and Le Mans. In general, the missions directed at England flew over the Channel Islands from Cherbourg and Caen although *Zerstörergeschwader* 76 was located in the Lille area. After only 6 weeks of combat against the RAF most of the Destroyer Groups had to be recalled to Germany for rest and recuperation because they had lost about 20 crews per Group, leaving only 10 to 12 experienced crews available for duty. On one occasion, a Group from Stavenger Norway was supposed to escort a bombing raid against Driffield in England but the bombing force was intercepted by Spitfires and bitter fighting resulted south of the mouth of the River Tyne. The Group lost its Commander, two Squadron Commanders and 12 crews and was completely torn to pieces. To provide a replacement, another Group that had been sent to Germany for recuperation had to be re-assigned to Norway to assume the bomber escort responsibility while operating in squadron and flight strength. When Hitler made the decision to attack Russia at the beginning of the Eastern Campaign, the Destroyer units were re-shuffled into *Schnellkampfgeschwaders* (Fast Bomber Wings) under the command of the General of Bomber Command. The chief functions of these units were to make attacks on airfields at low level, dropping 2kg fragmentation bombs and 50kg explosive bombs in support of the Army and tank spearheads. They also attacked enemy artillery and anti-aircraft gun emplacements.

Erich Hartmann

Gerhard Barkhorn

Josef "Pips" Priller

Walter Nowotny

Heinrich Ehrler

Joachim Müncheberg

Hans-Joachim Marseille

Heinrich Bartels

Messerschmitt Bf 109s

Focke-Wulf Fw 190s

In early 1942, a Fast Bomber Wing equipped with Bf 110s was transferred from the Eastern Front back into Germany at Lechfield to be re-equipped with the Me 210 an attempt at modernization. This move proved to be worse than ineffective because the newer aircraft was not a satisfactory combat machine from the point of view of the pilots who were assigned to fly it. A move was then made to reorganize several units into two mixed Destroyer Wings set up under Fighter Command. Each Wing had three Groups, two with Bf 110s and one with Bf 109s. All were used as ground attack units in Russia until an insufficient supply of replacement aircraft caused these units to collapse in the winter of 1942-43.

When the British introduced air to surface radar equipment into the aircraft of Coastal Command, German submarines passing through the Bay of Biscay began to suffer heavy losses. To give the submarines some relief, at least by day, the German Navy requested air support. A flight of Ju 88s from the Bomber Arm were set up to make attacks against shipping in the Atlantic, and this small unit was increased first to Squadron and then to Group strength by November of 1942. Operating in flights, the aircraft flew far out over the Atlantic and in addition operated from air bases around Lorient in France to combat Allied heavy bomber attacks on the U-boat bases when no Allied fighter escort accompanied the bombers.

These units scored initial successes against single multi-engine aircraft in the Bay of Biscay, but when RAF Coastal Command began to increase the number of Mosquito and Beaufighters making these attacks, the German Destroyers were forced to fly in double flight formations of eight aircraft for self-protection. The Ju 88s could perform fairly well against the Beaufighters, but they suffered heavy losses against the much faster Mosquito. Since an additional job of the *Zerstörers* was to protect German blockade runners, there were not enough on hand to do everything, so in early 1943 an additional Destroyer Wing was transferred from Russia to Brest as a stop gap measure. Still the Bf 110s were quite successful against bombers, but Spitfires flying down to Brest from England were more than a match for them and on one mission for example, nine out of twelve Bf 110s were shot down in the ocean North of the Sicily Islands.

As the war progressed, Allied fighter escorts penetrated deeper and deeper into the Bay of Biscay making the Destroyer operations increasingly difficult because of very high losses. Eventually, at the end of 1943 and the beginning of 1944, most of the *Zerstörer* units had to be transferred back into Germany to take part in the Defense of the *Reich*.

In 1941 in the Southern Theater of Operations, a Destroyer Group consisting of three Squadrons of Bf 110s and one Squadron of Do 17s operated throughout the Mediterranean Ocean. Their multiple assignments consisted of protecting the air and sea routes to Africa, attacking ground targets in Africa, conducting bombing raids against Malta, providing land and sea reconnaissance, and attacking enemy ship convoys. The Group was divided operationally with squadrons operating from Africa, Crete, and Sicily. This group which was obviously spread out very thinly had to be augmented by another in December 1942, but the new unit was equipped with Me 410s thus increasing operational efficiency.

Both of these Groups were very successful in combat although they were never used in a consistently concentrated manner for specific tasks, but were always overloaded by a wide variety of unrelated missions. As the Allies gradually gained air superiority, the Destroyers gradually began to suffer very heavy losses. Without ever having realized their potential, everywhere the Destroyers operated they had to be escorted by single-engine fighter aircraft even though the Bf 110 was equal in performance to the British Beaufighter that invariably met them.

During the battle for Tunisia in 1943, the Destroyers were used primarily to escort sea convoys and to cover air transport. Usually, the German convoys were attacked by enemy forces with fighter escort. So the *Zerstörers* also had to have the same escort in order to survive. The Air Transport units that flew terrible formations were often attacked from Africa by strong fighter forces and suffered devastating losses under these circumstances. When the *Luftwaffe* provided escort for the transport aircraft the Destroyers always flew close escort and the single-engine fighters provided top cover, but even this was not enough. As the war progressed the Destroyer Groups gradually were withdrawn to the Italian mainland, with one located in Naples and the other near Rome where, together with single-engine fighter units, they were used to attack the American heavy bomber formations. Although they scored some early successes against the B-17s and B-24s when using rockets, they suffered heavy losses because of inadequate fighter escort since the single-engine fighters were still needed in Sicily. However, the one Ju 88 Squadron remained in Greece on combat operations in the Aegean Sea against unescorted heavy bomber formations, and, under these conditions, they were quite successful.

In the summer of 1943, these two Groups were again transferred from Italy back into Germany because the American heavy bomber formations were penetrating deeper and deeper into the *Reich* in increasingly larger formations. In addition, another Group of Destroyers was recalled from the Russian front, and yet another from Brest and the Bay of Biscay. These groups were located at Wundsdorf and Hildesheim, later at Braunschweig, and finally at Konigsberg/Neumark while another Group conducted operations from Wels, near Linz, in Austria. One Group was transferred temporarily for three weeks to Constanza for the evacuation of the Crimea shooting down 28 Russian aircraft while losing only two of their own during escort missions. At the end of that short period they were again transferred to Wels to prepare for Defense of the *Reich*. In September 1943, a *Zerstörergeschwader* with three Groups was established by expanding a reconnaissance Squadron equipped with Bf 110's augmented by pilots and equipment from training school and night fighter units. These new Groups operated from airfields at Ansback, Wertheim, Ottingen, and later in Lepheim, Prague, Vienna, and Malacky in Czechoslovakia, but all were dissolved in February 1944 due to a lack of new aircraft and replacement crews.

The problems of the Destroyer Force, regardless of where assigned, resulted from the lack of high performance aircraft. Since the Bf 110 had to be flown at full throttle at a combat altitude of 25,000 feet, the crews found it very difficult to fly formation high up. In addition, when this aircraft was equipped with a forward firing 37mm cannon, it was very nose heavy, and could not turn well. This performance was not improved in the design of the Me 410 but this newer version did have one advantage. Its cannon could be fired at a range of 1,000 yards when a telescopic sight was used. One hit was usually enough to bring about a kill on a four-engine bomber. However, it was necessary to have extensive practice and excellent flying ability to shoot with the telescopic sight and the pilots had to fly into an extremely vulnerable position before firing in order to achieve a hit. The *Luftwaffe* High Command forced development of large caliber weapons against great resistance from the combat units, and this decision delayed the development and eventual use of rockets that had proved in combat to be much more successful. In addition, the experienced *Zerstörer* crews did not like the Me 410 even though it had about 65 mph more speed than the older Bf 110 because it could not turn as well and was extremely vulnerable to enemy fire. If it did actually catch fire, it was almost impossible to bail out successfully.

Initially, the *Luftwaffe* planned to use the *Zerstörer* Force in Defense of the *Reich* by employing the aircraft beyond the range of the American fighter escort in attacks against four-engine bombers. Since they would not become engaged in fighter versus fighter combat, the destroyer aircraft could be equipped with heavier armament, and their lack of maneuverability would not be operationally important. The mission plan was to use heavily armed destroyers to break up the heavy bomber formations by shooting at ranges outside the effective zone of defense and then to make attacks on individual stragglers with smaller caliber weaponry. Initially, these tactics brought considerable success as long as American fighter escort was not present, but every time the Destroyer Forces came into contact with enemy fighters, heavy losses resulted because both the Bf 110 and the Me 410 were inferior in every respect. When contact was actually made, only a defensive *Lufberry* Circle was helpful and this maneuver required superior flying ability, formations of at least 12 aircraft, and rearward firing weapons.

Eventually, Destroyers flew on operational missions in Defense of the *Reich* only when the heavy bombers were without fighter escort with single-engine fighters flying in formation with the attacking force. When early mission analysis indicated that the Destroyers should be able to make attacks on bombers which were not being escorted, Destroyer Squadrons located on airfields close to each other were given the start engines order over the commentary communications system and the aircraft took off in flights of four. Each Group assembled in a column of Squadrons while in a wide left hand turn and then flew directly to a Wing assembly point which was usually located over a prominent geographical point or over a radio beacon when the weather was bad.

At the Wing assembly point, the Groups formed into a long column of Groups, and, if the formations consisted of mixed types of aircraft, the Bf 110s flew ahead of the Me 410s. Once the enemy formations were sighted the Groups attacked one behind the other while closing range until the pilots were able to open fire with rockets at 800 to 1,000 yards. When all rockets had been fired the Groups closed formation again and attacked with cannon and machine guns. Some crews were able to score as many as eight victories in a single mission by using rockets that were fired on the order of the formation leader over the radio.

When attacking from either the front or the side of the enemy formations there was a tendency for the attackers to overshoot and when attacking from the rear the tendency was to undershoot, so the most practical form of attack was from dead astern because this method was, from the stand point of ballistics, perfect. When all combined attacks had been pressed home, the units resumed a column formation to return to home base. Until the end of 1943, the operational strength of Bf 110 Groups varied between 20 to 30 aircraft and the Me 410 units were held at 15 aircraft assigned. Losses averaged about 5 to 10 percent per mission and results against Allied heavy bombers were excellent.

Toward the end of 1943 the Destroyers came into contact with increasing numbers of American fighters, so the High Command decided to move all units back into Germany and to provide a fighter group for each *Zerstörer* Group, thus giving the Destroyer Force its own fighter escort. During this phase of the air battle, most of the Destroyer units removed the 21cm rocket launcher tubes in order to be more maneuverable when in contact with the enemy fighters. The fighter Groups flew close escort for the Destroyer units with two squadrons separated into individual flights flying on either side and behind the Destroyers with about 1,500 feet in altitude separation, so the entire formation appeared as a cross. The third Squadron in each Fighter Group flew top cover about 6,000 feet higher than the rest of the formation.

At first the fighters were forbidden to attack the bombers until it was determined that there were no American fighter escorts in the area then the formation leader could give the order to attack. However, the top cover Squadron was always excluded from attacking the bombers. The *Zerstörer* often attacked from head on while flying in a column of flights. Each flight would pass through formation after formation of bombers and then circle around to attack from behind while keeping the flights continuously in trail. These attacks required excellent cooperation between the fighters and the *Zerstörer*'s and losses remained within acceptable limited while the attackers scored considerable successes.

After March 1944, the American Fighter Escort was able to penetrate from the West as far as Stettin-Berlin-Munich and from the south as far as Vienna. These new assaults led to unbearable losses in the Destroyer Force because the German fighter escort was always involved in combat, and the pilots had all they could do to keep from getting themselves shot down let alone attacking the enemy bomber formations. For example, on March 16,1944 Allied fighters jumped the *Zerstörer* Force just as they were attacking the heavy bomber formations. There was no time to establish a *Lufberry* Circle and 26 aircraft were shot down and 10 belly-landed out of a total of 43 aircraft launched by *Zerstörergeschwader* 76 alone.

As a result of this specific action Fighter Command decided to use battle formations in which the Destroyer Groups with their escort fighters would make combined concentrated attacks without restrictions. Initially, this new tactic was successful, but soon after each successful attack on the bomber stream, the entire German formation became so spread out that the American fighter escort was usually able to attack Destroyers that had usually broken down into flights or four or even individual aircraft. During the first American raid on Berlin in March 1944, the battle formations were led by a Wing Commander and his flight staff. They were followed by formations of Bf 110s and Me 410s in trail with single-engine fighters bringing up the rear. Assembling this large formation took a very long time and it was extremely difficult to control them all by radio communication. Altogether over 200 aircraft of which 70 were Destroyers were massed for attack against the heavy bomber formation. During this one battle alone one Destroyer Group was destroyed and another suffered extremely heavy losses because they were surprised by a large number of Allied escort fighters.

In May 1944, several more Destroyer Groups were converted to the Me 410s, but this did not solve the problem confronting the *Zerstörer* Forces because the American fighter escort became stronger as the German fighter force became weaker. Success in the air became a matter of skillful vectoring or being lucky enough to meet the heavy bomber formations when the escorting fighters were not in a position to defend them. This did happen occasionally and once during a raid directed against the oil refineries at Stettin, *Zerstörergeschwader* 26 scored 15 victories for only 2 losses.

Again in July 1944, 12 Me 410s shot down 8 American four-engine bombers with no losses during an attack on Budapest. *Zerstörer* Group I in the area of Budapest Vienna-Munich scored a large number of victories while sustaining very few losses during this period. Eventually this unit was a victim of a surprise attack by Mustangs during a raid on Weiner Neustad and lost 13 out of 26 Bf 110s that were committed to battle. On this same mission *Zerstörer* Group I from *Geschwader* 76 began an interception from Vienna with 12 Bf 110s and in climbing up to an assembly point on the Danube to the West were surprised by Lockheed Lightnings and lost a total of ten combat crews. After these heavy battles both *Zerstörergeschwader* 26 and 76 were converted to single-engine fighters at the end of June 1944 and this action had to have been a secretly desired wish of the remaining Destroyer crews at that time.

Most of the *Luftwaffe* authorities felt that the Destroyer Force had its place in history even though these units were doomed to failure from the start because the aircraft they flew were inferior to a well equipped enemy, especially one with air superiority. Since the Destroyers were used for so many purposes, attention was always diverted from the original mission and the result was a complete dissipation of effort. In addition, so much attention was given to the development and operational use of the Destroyer units that the *Luftwaffe* failed to develop a suitable long-range single-engine fighter force in time to influence the outcome of the air war.

Still, in 1943, the Destroyers almost fulfilled their promise, but they missed having a decisive role in the Defense of the *Reich* because of the superiority of the Allied Fighter Forces. They failed in part because the Me 210 was a great technical failure and the Me 410 came into operational use about one year too late. The Fw 154 was supposed to add to the capability of the Me 410 Destroyer units because it had better performance, but production was canceled before any large quantities came into operational use. The Dornier 335 could have been a suitable Destroyer, but the High Command committed this machine to fast bombers, night fighters, reconnaissance aircraft, and, lastly, to the role of Destroyer, thus squandering this great asset on a host of unrelated tasks.

Despite all the mistakes made in formulation, planning, and operation the *Zerstörer* Force achieved remarkable results even in the most difficult times through high morale and the courage of its personnel. These achievements could never have been accomplished had it not been for the extremely high caliber of the formation leaders and their aircrews.

CHAPTER EIGHT

Missions

Every fighter pilot that has ever enjoyed the thrill of flying a powerful and beautiful machine designed only to engage and destroy enemy aircraft thinks that a fighter sweep is the most original and the most natural type of combat mission. In his element the fighter pilot can determine and utilize all the advantageous factors of aerial combat especially in fighter sweeps even though they are not an end but only a means to an end. Fighter aircraft have been used during various wars to combat enemy reconnaissance, to spot artillery, to sweep over the battle field tactical area in order to combat enemy fighter-bombers and other ground attack aircraft, to lure enemy fighters into battle, clear the combat areas, secure aerial flanks, and to destroy enemy aircraft where ever possible. Fighters have also been used over enemy airfields to weaken anti-aircraft defenses, they have been used to engage enemy fighter escort in battle thus diverting them from their escort mission, and, finally, they have been used to attack ground targets on fighter sweep missions.

During peace time prior to the war, German tactical regulations made little or no mention of fighter sweeps although these were the primary aerial missions of World War I. In Spain, however, more than fifty percent of all combat missions flown were fighter sweeps. Even the ground attack squadrons were quite successful with fighter sweep missions because the combat areas were well defined and the Germans always had air superiority. In Poland and in the French campaign in 1940 fighter sweeps were used to force the enemy into the air as well. It was necessary to have friendly forces in the air in the event the enemy conducted patrols on his own because the aircraft warning system was never good enough to allow time for scramble starts once the enemy appeared. The German High Command started the Battle of Britain with fighter sweeps because they hoped to reduce the RAF fighter strength to the point where *Luftwaffe* bombers would be able to operate without opposition. They also used fighters to escort small formations of decoy bombers in hopes that RAF fighters would be lured into combat with the wrong target and then destroyed.

Fighter sweeps were especially popular in Russia because they were quite successful and they were conducted whenever there were enough aircraft in commission to permit a sweep in strength. On the Mediterranean and African fronts fighter sweeps were seldom launched because the fighter forces were always over-loaded by a great variety of missions that had higher priority. Still, Galland's Me 262 Fighter Wing flew sweeps right up to the end of the war against the Allies. Hermann Göring and his staff never did understand any reason for fighter sweeps because they insisted that all air operations must have definite objectives. Thus fighter sweeps were only permitted when there were no other kinds of offensive missions to be flown, and then the Fighter Command, Divisions, Corps, *Jafu*'s or other headquarters only gave orders to fly fighter sweeps without specifying strength, area to be patrolled, or times over targets. When the commands did give permission for fighter sweeps, the Wings usually added implementing instructions such as the number of aircraft to be used, the time of take off, and the areas in which the fighters were to operate. The altitudes were left to the judgment of the individual leaders. After each mission was completed the Groups reported the time of take off and landing and the number of victories if any to higher headquarters by telephone. The number of aircraft involved on each sweep depended upon aircraft availability, weather conditions, potential enemy reaction and the depth of penetration into enemy territory. In Russia sweeps were flown in flight or slightly larger strengths. In France they were flown only in Group strength, during the Battle of Britain only in Group or Wing strength and during the Defense of the *Reich* and the Ardennes Offensive in the largest sized units possible and with the greatest strength available were flown.

In all cases Group Commanders usually briefed their own flying personnel and the briefings were kept short and simple.

It was usually left to the formation leader to plan each mission by
taking advantage of all possible conditions such as the position of the
sun, cloud cover, moment of attack and time of break off. Since the outcome of all engagements between enemy and friendly fighters usually
depended on who saw who first, relative strength of the foes played only
a minor role providing the technical performance of the aircraft involved
was approximately equal and the pilots had equal experience and training. The best advantage lay in surprise, then came position, technical
performance, the ability of the pilots to shoot accurately, cohesion in formation, and finally, relative strength of the opposing formations. For example the Germans were almost always outnumbered in Russia, but they
still emerged victorious right up to the end of the war because they used
better equipment, better tactics and better formations and the pilots were
confident of their superiority. However, in the Battle of Britain the Germans felt that they had better tactics and flying ability, but the ability of
the British to position their fighters for attack gave them the necessary
advantage to win.

Fighter sweeps were conducted almost the same as any other type of
mission except that it was necessary to take off and assemble as rapidly
as possible (because of the limited fuel the fighters carried) so all aircraft
started engines at the same time in order to rapidly assemble for take off.
German pilots did not like airfields with paved runways because the number of aircraft that could take off in formation was limited by the width of
the runway, whereas it was possible to make formation takeoffs with entire squadrons on grass or sod surfaces. It was necessary to have the entire group in formation after one circuit of the field or in approximately
three minutes after take off and regardless of the size of the formation,
the lead Squadron departed first. Units flew in a rather wide-open formation with elements stepped up until they entered the combat area when
the formation closed up slightly climbing to gain altitude. Since altitude
was a most important advantage formation leaders tried to jump the enemy from above while achieving the element of surprise if at all possible.

In a dog fight, climbing ability was always used to advantage although top cover aircraft always dived into combat to support those who
were first engaged. It was always necessary for the top cover to regain

altitude after a fight in order to attack again with an altitude advantage if need be, and this usually prevented enemy fighters from re-entering the fight at superior altitudes. It was a cardinal rule that flights and elements should not break up in combat, but must try to remain together for mutual support. Formation leaders could order their formations to break off combat and return to base for a variety of reasons, but when pilots broke off individual combat by split-essing or dive away the results were usually fatal. Even still this tactic happened more and more frequently as poorly trained pilots joined the units and as the experience level of the leaders deteriorated. Lack of discipline in battle was always a sign of an inferior fighter force caused by inadequate replacements that lacked a sense of achievement, lacked training, and, above all, lacked morale. None of these deficiencies could be corrected by punishment or by direct order, but success always resulted in an increase of self-confidence. Toward the end of the war almost every German formation broke up, but at least the elements and flights tried to stay together. Aircraft returning to land usually had no organization and always consisted of stragglers trying to land all over Germany especially during the last days of the Defense of the *Reich*.

Fighter sweeps were most popular and profitable during the Battle of Britain, but the changing patterns of attack by the Allied Air Armadas outmoded the fighter sweep and forced many changes in the method of operation of the *Luftwaffe* Fighter Forces because they were forced to shift to the defensive. Each time the Allies tried something new the *Luftwaffe* was forced to alter mission profiles, briefings and operational patterns. Although the German High Command had certainly benefited from the experiences of the Battle of Britain, the lessons they learned from the RAF were made obsolete by the sheer mass of the Allied attacks. The air war probably reached its highest intensity as far as the German Fighter Force was concerned during the Allied raids that proceeded the first attack in strength on Berlin. During this period prior to the invasion, the *Luftwaffe* was able to mount very heavy attacks on the Allied heavy bomber formations, and each operational mission became extremely complex. At the time a typical day in the *Luftwaffe* was entirely different than the same day was to the Allies. All ranks of the *Luftwaffe* were forced into a completely different life than they had enjoyed during the Battle of Britain simply because they had to shift to the defensive.

A mission conducted by the 8th Air Force against Frankfort only October 4th, 1943 was typical of most missions launched by the Allied heavy bombers prior to the invasion. On that day in Germany the weather officers had indications that conditions were favorable to the Allies, so heavy bomber attacks were expected and could come from the South as well as the West. In addition excellent weather conditions existed over the entire *Reich* and thus were suitable for the *Luftwaffe* defensive forces also. At 5:30 in the morning Wing Commanders were contacted by their Division Commanders who passed down plans for the day from the High Command through the *Jagdkorps* and the *Luftflotte* that read as follows:

"Today on the basis of weather reports, enemy attacks from the south and the west are to be expected. Weather for defense is ideal. Your Wing will be used to combat any enemy formations from the West, but if the enemy only penetrates as far as the occupied zones of France, Belgium and Holland, you will be expected to attack any strikes from the South should they develop. Ready times will be directed as usual when the Listening Service picks up any bombers assembling over England or Italy, and your Wing will go into 15 minute readiness at that time."

After receiving this message, all Wing Commanders were expected to relay these instructions to their Groups and all subordinate commanders were in turn expected to hold pre-briefings for all pilots. These briefings always took place in the unit briefing room with the Wing Commander presiding. In addition to the pilots, the briefings were always attended by the Squadron Commander the Technical or Engineering Officer, the Weather Officer, and the Operations Officer. On this day at 6:45 a.m., the pilots assembled and the strength was reported to the Group Commander. Physical exercise drills were given with the torso bare, and the exercises included body bends, twisting exercises, arm exercises, knee bends and a short run. At 7:15 the briefing began. The Meteorologist always gave the first briefing by drawing on a large map with crayons as he predicted the possibility of attacks from both the west and south. He described the direction of any frontal activity and the condition of areas where fog could be expected, areas of dangerously low clouds, and heavy rain, adding where it would be possible to detour around any weather. He added predictions for the next day as he concluded with winds aloft, and the altitude at which icing could be expected. Since the weather changed quite rapidly at this time of year, any weather that had recently passed over England and the Low Countries could usually be expected to pass over Germany shortly after, much to the disadvantage of the defending forces.

When the weather officer had concluded his briefing, the Technical Officer was called upon to provide the Commander with a chart of serviceable aircraft, and at the same time to discuss any technical problems concerning the aircraft that might be valuable to the pilots. He was followed in turn by the Communications Officer who provided information on those aircraft which were equipped with Very High Frequency radios which were used for command and control between all formation leaders and the ground radio direction stations. He also mentioned any special instructions from any part of the entire communications network.

Following these presentations, the Group Commander gave the operational briefing according to the instructions he had received from the Wing:

"Assuming that one attack is expected from the North, the Group will lead the *Gefechtsverband* as this mission actually materializes. The Group Staff will lead with one Squadron on the left, another on the right, and a third behind in trail. Attacks will be made from head on. Remember to approach from the same altitude as the bombers, aim well, don't shoot from too great a range, and be sure to pull out and side-slip away after making the attack. We will assemble after each attack according to position of the sun providing the enemy fighter escort does not interfere. A second Group will follow us and a third Group will provide cover for us. Our Wing will assemble at 25,000 feet and a second Wing will assemble at 30,000 feet with light fighters over the Dummer Sea. I will lead the entire attacking force and my Deputy will be the Commander of the 7th Squadron. Oldenburg, Delmhorst, and Rothenbur are to be used for intermediate landings after the mission. All are well supplied with mechanics, refueling and repair facilities. Senior pilots who arrive at the recovery fields first are responsible for immediate servicing of all aircraft and they will report the number of aircraft available for a second possible mission to the Division immediately. Make sure all aircraft are returned to flight readiness as soon as possible so you can all return to our base here. Take care on landing at the intermediate airfields and be sure to watch out for enemy fighters and bomb craters. Disperse your aircraft immediately after landing and camouflage them. Senior pilots will go to field operations to report to the Division how many aircraft and pilots have landed, what their victories have been, and how many are ready to start again. All others will remain with their aircraft until released."

After these comments the papers of all pilots were checked and all were issued emergency packets consisting of burn bandages, salve, and rubber tourniquets for arterial bleeding. Pilots were instructed to return to base by train if forced to make a crash landing bringing their aircraft radios back with them. If they made a forced landing and their aircraft was intact they were instructed to make arrangements for having it guarded. If hospitalized they were to ask the doctor to notify their units as soon as possible.

To reinforce the briefing, the Commander had one or another of the pilots repeat all special subjects such as assembly points, airfields, intermediate landing fields and emergency procedures.

Often a Squadron Commander would conduct the briefing under the supervision of the Group Commander because some day the Squadron C.O. might have to replace the Group C.O., but this was not the case for this mission. At the end of the briefing, pilots were transported to the unit dispersal area where their aircraft were standing ready for take off. At this time the Squadron Commanders assigned aircraft and appointed flight and element leaders. Since the weather was fair (indicating that an attack would come) the Group was on a thirty minute readiness and the pilots were not allowed to leave the field. Usually, the dispersal was quite livable with a small kitchen, recreational areas, and washing facilities often made from external fuel tanks. Until the order came for take off every pilot stayed close to the immediate area where his individual machine was parked.

By this time the Wing Headquarters had been in full operation since dawn because an enemy attack seemed likely, and continuous information had been given out to the Groups concerning the changes that had been made in organization and operation for the day. Call signs had been established down through the chain of command to the formation and deputy formation leaders. In addition, the Division Commentary has been in operation since 8:20 a.m. giving out enemy progress reports as the Allied Bomber formations rendezvoused and began to cross over the English Coast. Over England all three American Bomber Divisions had been airborne since about 4:00 a.m. 361 heavies were now on their way to targets in the Frankfort area. The Division Commentary in Germany was following the progress of these formations as they headed east over the Scheld Estuary at 9:00 a.m. At that time the Wing was given instructions to go into a three-minute readiness state and shortly thereafter instructions were issued for condition *"Sitzbereitschaft"* meaning that the pilots were to sit in their aircraft. Now that all pilots were in their cockpits around the edge of the field ready to start engines. Loud speakers located throughout the entire air base were broadcasting the commentary. The enemy bomber formations had continued due east for a period of time, but just West of the Rhine, they had turned Southeast toward the Rhine-Main Industrial Complex surrounding the city of Frankfort.

In the meantime, the Division Commander had held repeated conversations with the Wing Commanders and the *Jagdkorps* and had decided to use all the Wings in readiness against the bombers approaching from the West since there were no signs of any attack coming from the South. Around 9:40 a.m. the leading bomber formation was Southwest of Cologne over the Eifel area, so the Wing got orders to start engines. All three Groups made a scramble start, assembling over their own airfields at 3,000 to 6,000 feet in 6 to 10 minutes while heading to the Wing assembly point. Upon arrival the Wing Commander who had been the first to take off formed the attacking formation or the *Gefechtsverband*. The assembly altitude had been previously established at 10,000 feet to keep under any possible cloud formations, and it had been specified that all units would be in formation no later than twenty minutes after the time of take off of the Groups.

As soon as the formation set course for its objective, the Wing Commander informed the Division that assembly had been completed and the formation was on its way to intercept. The Division in turn gave the order, "Set course at 320 and climb to a combat altitude of 25,000 feet." The Wing straightened out of the turn that had been used to assemble all aircraft, heading out on course as the formation leader throttled back to allow the rest of the formation to close in behind him. The close escort divided with one half going to the left and the other to the right of the *Sturmgruppen* aircraft which were especially heavily armed and armored to give the pilots the capability of pressing home very close attacks. The top cover took position 3,000 to 6,000 feet above the whole formation that was by that time stacked up from front to rear. All aircraft climbed at 220 mph indicated air speed while climbing at 600 to 900 feet per minute. During a climb it was mandatory to maintain radio discipline because the Division sent up continuous commentary describing the enemy location and progress. Since the Division knew where the friendly fighter formation was located in relation to the enemy bombers, the Formation leader was continually advised of his position by the use of codes and numbers (to reduce the possibility of the enemy listening service betraying the activities of the fighters) as the Division prepared to direct the battle formation into the attack.

The formation continued to climb as directed toward the Rhine-Main area and over Wurzberg they reached an altitude of 23,000 feet where the leader could see contrails ahead and to the left. Shortly after, he was able to see flak from anti-aircraft weapons firing from the Frankfort area. In the meantime the formation leader had been advised by the Division to expect the arrival of formations of *Zerstörer* aircraft which would be approaching the bomber stream from behind and below in order to make rocket and cannon attacks. At 10:50 he was able to make visual contact with the first enemy bomber formations, and, after passing this information along to the Division, he received the order to attack and was released from ground control.

Unknown to the Germans the British had produced paper external fuel tanks which could contain 108 gallons of fuel which they made available to the USAAF 8th Fighter Command. These tanks were being delivered in small quantities and the 56th Fighter Group (the first Group to go operational with the Republic P-47 Thunderbolt) equipped with them was on the way to rendezvous with the lead box of American bombers some 325 miles from their home base in England. This was by far the deepest penetration by Allied Fighter aircraft at the time, so the pilots had been cautioned to use the engine controls prudently if they were to complete their phase of the escort for the heavy bomber formations.

Until 10:50, the German formation leader had made no contact with enemy escort fighters, so he had given the order to attack a formation of about 60 heavy bombers which had just dropped their bombs and were turning away from the target area. The *Sturmgruppen* together with a large *Zerstörer* force was just beginning to make attacks on the bottom box of bombers when the American fighters appeared on the scene. Looking down, the Group leader of the 56th Group observed forty plus twin-engine Bf 110s approaching for a surprise attack and suddenly the German crews were in turn surprised to find USAAF Thunderbolts bearing down on them. The heavy and unwieldy *Zerstörer*s had no opportunity to lob rockets into the bomber formations and they were no match for the single-engine fighters.

A Thunderbolt pilot reported thus on the battle that followed in his combat report:

"While flying in large S turns over the bomber formations I noticed what appeared to be a small box of bombers at a lower altitude trailing the main formation. These aircraft were in essentially the same formation as the "Big Friendlies" but somehow they didn't look right. I decided to drop down to investigate, and found to my surprise that there were from 40 to 60 twin-engine aircraft closing in on the "friendlies." After calling the Group Leader, I went down taking my entire flight with me. We came boiling up behind the enemy aircraft which turned out to be Bf 110s.

I let go at the first one I saw. With terrific closing speed, I was within 500 feet of the enemy when my shots ripped him to pieces many large parts flew from the wings and tail, and both engines caught fire almost immediately, causing-him to dive out of control. Simultaneously others in the Squadron had started to fire and the German formation was splitting up in every direction. As I broke away from my attack I pulled up in time to see several enemy aircraft above and in front of me. I was so confused and excited that I started to take snap shots at every enemy aircraft I could see even though I didn't have a chance of hitting them. Suddenly, I realized that I would squirt away all my ammunition if I didn't manage to get into a good firing position behind just one of the enemy, so I pulled out of the fight to find a German in proper position to attack. Off to my right I saw a single Bf 110 letting down underneath the B-17s obviously on his way back home for a landing. Diving behind him, I opened fire at close range and at a great closing speed. There were many sparks at the bullets struck home causing large pieces to fall away from the aircraft. At this time my element leader called to inform me that he had lost me in the fight.

I broke away, only to spot another Bf 110 heading 90 from the friendlies in a gradual dive toward Frankfort. With full throttle, I closed astern and let loose. As soon as the shots began to pepper him he rolled over on his back, performing a split S maneuver so as to head for the ground vertically. I didn't want to let him get away and split-essed with him firing down vertically until I observed many hits all over his machine which by this time had begun to disintegrate. My overtake speed in the dive caused me to pass over him, and I pulled back into level flight position but had lost my wingman.

The bomber stream had progressed many miles ahead of my position, and I found I was alone. I could still hear the sounds of fighting ahead, and at full throttle I sought to catch up with the rest of the fight. For the last time, I saw one more German heading in the opposite direction heading back into Germany. It was a simple thing to make a 180 turn into position for attack. I really clobbered this guy until I ran out of ammunition. Many pieces had fallen away from the Bf 110 and its right engine was on fire when I saw the enemy pilot leap over the side and a few moments later pull his parachute ripcord. Then, without ammunition and alone in the sky, I had to get home."

After the *Zerstörers* had broken off from the attack on the B-17s, the German fighters tried to attack various bomber formations, but they became involved in aerial combat with large numbers of Thunderbolts until the battle reached the vicinity of the Moselle River. At about 11:30 the Germans broke off aerial combat. The few German flights still in operation together with all aircraft flying alone were directed to land in the vicinity of Mannheim. By 12:00 all had landed in the prescribed area without interference from enemy fighters. On these intermediate airfields each pilot went to the field operations room where he gave a short report of his mission and all formation leaders called the nearest responsible fighter command headquarters to give a short report by priority telephone. After all the aircraft had been serviced with fuel and ammunition, the fighter command gave orders that all aircraft were to return to their bases since there appeared to be no more enemy activity. Besides they seemed to be too far away to be attacked by a second mission.

Second missions did not lead to much success anyway because it was very difficult to form the pilots and aircraft into efficient fighting units when they had landed on many different airfields. After all had landed at home bases, the formation leaders gave operational reports which included victories and losses to higher headquarters. The Wing and Group Commanders attempted to critique each mission as soon as possible in order to generate a clear picture of the entire combat mission while it was still fresh in mind. On this day the major topic of concern was the deep penetration of the American fighters which portended major problems for the German fighter forces in the future and the report of this discussion was made by telephone and confirmed later in writing. Because of the gravity of the situation, the Wing and Group Commanders held a conference telephone conversation with the Division Commander to discuss the results and the object lessons to be learned from this engagement in hopes of coming up with new ideas to improve tactics. In the event a new tactic was devised, or in the event the enemy used new equipment or formations, it was always customary for the Commanders to discuss these matters with the General of the Fighter Forces or with the Inspector of Day Fighters.

When all reports of the engagement were in, 16 heavy bombers had been shot down including 4 B-24s that were on a diversionary flight. The Allies claimed 56 German aircraft had been destroyed by return fire from the B-17s, and the American Fighter Pilots claimed 19 enemy aircraft had been shot down with one loss to the USAAF side. However, actual German losses amounted to 28 aircraft, 21 of which were twin-engine *Zerstörers*. Even at that, it was a considerable blow to the *Luftwaffe* especially in view of the deep penetration of the Thunderbolts.

CHAPTER NINE

Fighters Up

Before World War II, the German single-engine fighters did not have the range required for strategic bombing, so peacetime doctrine required bomber formations to conduct maneuvers without fighter escort. When the *Zerstörer* units were established in 1937 and equipped with fast bombers such as the Dornier 17 and the Heinkel 111 the Germans decided that bombers of the future would always be able to out distance the fighters. In Germany the fighter forces were using old, slow Arado 65s and 68s as well as the Heinkel 51 and so the bombers could easily out distance them in both speed and range. In Spain, the Republican Forces, especially the Russians, always employed fighter escort for their bombers, and this discovery caused great consternation in *Luftwaffe* circles. When the Bf 109 eventually went into combat in Spain, it reversed *Luftwaffe* thinking, but still no real technical effort was directed toward bringing the range of fighter aircraft into line with the bombers. The Germans never did develop any strategic aerial warfare concept in which bombers and fighters would operate together in the day light against enemy industrial targets.

Instead, *Luftwaffe* planners maintained that the twin-engine *Zerstörer*s would always have performance equal to or better than modern single engine fighters. In actual practice, however, the Bf 110 was able to perform adequately in Poland and in France. In the Battle of Britain, this aircraft suffered the defeat that had been predicted all along by the proponents of single-engine fighters. As a result of this debacle the role of escort was assigned to the single-engine fighter force even though all the aircraft had inadequate range and endurance. The people responsible for the development felt that the deficiencies of the twin-engine aircraft could be improved by increasing technical performance and this philosophy led to the construction and series production of the Me 210 which later was further developed into the Me 410. Excluding serious problems of construction, these aircraft could never have been equal to modern single-engine fighters, and attention should have focused on extending the range and increasing the over-all performance of the entire single-engine fighter force instead.

Until the external drop tank was introduced, nothing was done to increase range. In fact, just the opposite occurred almost by accident. As the power of the Bf 109 engines increased because of technical improvements, the fuel consumption increased and so the range decreased because the quantity of internal fuel remained the same. Still, this machine, as well as others in the same category, was called upon to perform close escort, escort cover for bombers, sweeps to clear the approach to and departure from target areas, and combined escort for vulnerable single and twin-engine fighters. The *Luftwaffe* High Command had a concept of close escort that absolutely prohibited fighter pilots to allow air battles to lure them away from the immediate vicinity of the bomber formations. Usually, both twin-engine and single-engine fighters were assigned to protect certain bomber formations, and this was always done in at least Squadron strength. However, this type of escort was generally ineffective because the fighters were always on the defensive since the defenders had more possibilities for attack and time was always in their favor. In addition, because of the slow speed of their formations, the fighters had to continually weave back and forth and to change altitude frequently just to stay in the general vicinity of the bombers. When the bomber crews could see fighters from their cockpits they felt that they were being adequately protected and they had no interest in any combat that took place outside their immediate vicinity. From the standpoint of the fighter pilots this was never satisfactory because a roving escort was a prerequisite for keeping enemy fighters at a distance. The Allies had to go through the same experiences later in order to learn exactly the same lesson.

Since the bomber crews always complained when they could not see fighters, the *Luftwaffe* issued strict directives providing for close escort which in turn prevented the fighter force from protecting the bombers satisfactorily. However, high morale and *esprit de corps* sometimes intervened and only a part of the fighters carried out their difficult escort jobs with strict discipline while the rest ranged far and wide seeking to destroy the enemy. Still, the cooperation between bombers and fighters was especially effective when a specific bomber unit would work for a long time in cooperation with certain fighter units and, between them they could work out problems caused by their opposing interests and demands. Initially, in the Battle of Britain, twin-engine fighters were able to conduct attacks alone successfully, but eventually the RAF recognized the substandard performance of the Destroyers. When the RAF took advantage of their weaknesses, Destroyer losses became unbearable. They could no longer escape from combat and were always forced to take defensive *Lufberry* maneuvers just to survive. Eventually, the Destroyers could no longer be used to escort bomber formations because they, themselves, required escort. Thus, they only added to the burden of the single-engine fighter force.

When individual bombers fell out of formation because they had mechanical trouble or were damaged during combat, it was necessary for the escort fighters to provide close cover for the imperiled aircraft. Often, this tactic was successful because the main force of RAF fighters would be directed at the larger formations of attacking bombers and the escort covering the retiring singles would not be worth an attack. As time went on during the Battle of Britain, even the *Luftwaffe* High Command began to realize that close escort could never be successful against energetic and strong fighter attacks. Eventually after repeated demands by the German fighter formation leaders, the High Command decided that the fighter forces would provide both close escort and escort cover provided by Squadrons or small Groups flying about 3,000 to 6,000 feet higher than the bombers and well off to one side. Their mission was to disrupt the approaching enemy fighter formations before they could get close to the bombers fighting until they were out of position to attack the bomber formation effective. They were to immediately return to the bombers and continue escort cover after breaking off engagement. They were also required to help the close escort fighters should the enemy break through the cover by surprise to attack the bombers from the front or below. Regardless of the violence of the air battle, it was necessary for the escort cover to remain with the bombers all the way in and out of the target area.

The assigned number of close escort and escort cover aircraft depended on the strength of the bomber formations as well as the strength and size of the expected enemy fighter opposition. At best there should have been a one to one relationship. All aircraft equipped with radios were to remain in communication with each other although at the start of the Battle of Britain many aircraft did not have the necessary radio gear to maintain any contact with one another. The Germans never did have enough radio equipment right up until the end of the war, so many pilots went into combat (and to their death) without the ability to talk or even listen to what was going on in the air. Initially, the German Air Force tried to communicate with Very Pistol signals and smoke flares, but this approach proved to have no value what so ever.

In special situations the escort cover could be released to strafe ground targets on the way home, but this was done only when it was known for sure that no further contact with enemy fighters could be expected. The *Luftwaffe* judged the success of the close escort and escort-cover missions by the way bomber formations were protected and by the number of losses they suffered. Victories by escort fighters were always included in evaluating the success of any over-all effort, but these figures were often distorted by the heat of the battle and down played in any evaluation. If the escort fighters had been allowed to go after the RAF fighter force as their primary mission, the entire outcome of the Battle of Britain would have been different. The RAF fighter force would probably have been weakened to the point where the German bomber formations would have attacked targets practically without opposition.

Surprisingly, the USAAF Fighter Command had to go through this same learning process. Initially, it was considered almost a court martial offense to leave the bomber stream to attack enemy fighter aircraft. Even though it was virtually impossible to break up any enemy mass attack once it had been committed to an assault on a specific box of bombers, it took a long time to recognize that these attacks could be broken up great distances away from the battle area providing fighters were allowed to roam at will to search for assembling German aircraft. However, by the time the Allies were learning this lesson, the GAF was putting into practice all the lessons they had learned from the British during the Battle of Britain regarding how best to attack large enemy bomber formations.

The *Luftwaffe* considered fighter sweeps to be of value in clearing the approach to target areas prior to penetration of the bomber formations but only providing there were enough fighter aircraft available. If the strength and tactics of the enemy fighter forces were diagnosed properly, this kind of attack proved to be very successful. However, the sweeping aircraft had to be scheduled to arrive over the target at the proper time while scouring the approach route ahead of the bombers in hopes to engage every fighter formation the enemy put into the air. In this manner it was expected that most of the enemy formations would either be broken up or at least kept away from the immediate vicinity of the bombers.

On this kind of sweep, even the escort fighters were allowed to enter any fight, but the sweeping fighters were directed to press on to the target area regardless of any aerial combat that might intervene. After bombs were away the fighters were allowed to begin withdrawing from the target area but only when rear cover was established to defend against hordes of pursuing enemy fighters. Missions of the sweeping fighters had a two-fold purpose; they were expected to shoot down the enemy and yet keep as many enemy fighters away from the attacking bomber formations is possible. This type of mission always proved fruitful and was by far the most popular with fighter pilots in general.

German fighter escort was seriously effected by limited endurance and short range during the Battle of Britain. The fighters always had to rendezvous with the bombers on the Eastern Channel Coast, and the bombers could cause no delays. In addition, the route to and from the target had to be made over the shortest possible distance, so the British always knew what the Germans were up to. As a result these strikes always suffered because there was little or no element of surprise. If anything unusual happened the fighters were not able to return to their home bases after a mission and often had to land on a beach or in the water because they were out of fuel. Even though drop-able fuel tanks were introduced during the Battle of Britain, the still short range of escorting fighters prevented the Germans from launching any really large bomber streams and, instead, the Bomber wings were forced to attack their targets in small string formations which were very difficult to defend. There was no way to surprise the RAF with variations or tricks of any kind. When specific bomber formations crossed the coast to rendezvous with the appropriate fighter forces, they were scheduled so closely in point and time that they would often rendezvous with the wrong elements while leaving others insufficiently covered or lacking cover entirely. As the winter weather closed in late in 1940, the situation deteriorated because the bombers and fighters could no longer rendezvous above the clouds since there were solid clouds at all altitudes. The Germans had not yet developed radar nor had they established any ground to air fighter control procedures that were effective because the fighters were out of communication range. The net effect of all these problems caused heavy bomber and fighter losses, and the fact that the Do 17 and the He 111 did not have enough defensive fire power and could be crippled easily only served to complicate the problem. Whenever the striking force encountered bad weather it suffered very heavy additional losses. If decisions were made to attack targets beyond the range of fighters, the strikes had to be made at night just to keep the losses within some sort of acceptable limits.

On the Southern Front, especially during the Battle of Malta, the German fighter forces were so limited in number that it was not possible to provide bomber strikes with both close escort and escort cover. The GAF tried various types of escort as the tactical situation and number of aircraft available would permit, but strikes on Malta always resulted in heavier and heavier losses because the fighter defenses on the island became stronger and stronger. Whenever the *Luftwaffe* tried to escort transport aircraft in the Mediterranean, they always met with failure because the transports flew at such slow speed that it was virtually impossible to protect them. The small fighter forces that could be launched always encountered very heavy enemy fighter reaction. Throughout the war, the *Luftwaffe* was never able to devise any new or significant tactics on the Southern Front.

The air battle on the Eastern Front was an entirely different matter, and, over the course of the years, the *Luftwaffe* developed high standards of technical achievement as well as excellent operational tactics. Still, they never did get around to conducting strategic bombing operations that would have been of great assistance to the *Wermacht*. As it was, fighter escort for any kind of bombing missions was carried out in a most primitive manner. A few fighters would simply attach themselves to the bomber formations as they passed over fighter bases and then escort them to the target and back. When they got back to the front lines, the fighters would break off and conduct fighter sweeps independently. The Russian fighters usually refused to attack even though the German bombers were lightly armed and protected by little or no escort because they had not developed the capability to make any sort of disciplined attacks. Usually, the German bombers encountered only a few courageous Russian lone wolves who would dive into the bomber formations with great skill and cunning.

Throughout the campaign in the East, four fifths of the fighter combat was waged over the battle area in support of the Army. When the *Luftwaffe* made bomber strikes in support of the troops, there were usually many less fighters than bombers. When long penetration raids were launched, they did make an effort to provide an equal number of bombers and fighters. Initially, there were no radar installations in Russia so fighter control was nonexistent. When this capability was eventually introduced, it was still not very effective because the German war machine was constantly in retreat. However, the Listening Service was very good and always proved to be useful during air battles because the Russians were not given to silence during moments of stress. When the *Luftwaffe* was directed to conduct supply and support missions to surrounded areas such as Stalingrad, Demjansk, Crimea Cholm and so forth, it was very difficult for the fighter arm because the transport aircraft were so slow and the Russians had so many weapons directed at the entrapped German ground forces. However, when airfields were available within the area of entrapment, the fighters actually landed right along with the transports so they could resume escort as soon as the larger aircraft started back to their home bases.

Initially, the Ju 87 dive-bomber aircraft were largely flown by fighter pilots, so they took on a special character more closely related to fighters than to bombers. Even at the beginning of the Battle of Britain the Ju 87 was obsolete because it was so slow in level flight and even in dives. Inadequately armed from both front and rear, the *Luftwaffe* was forced to take them out of combat very early on. When the Germans lost air superiority in Africa, the Stuka could only be employed when there was fighter cover and even then the losses were extremely heavy. In Russia conditions were different, so the Ju 87 was used right up to the end of the war. Surprisingly, less Stukas were shot down by Russian fighters than were destroyed by anti-aircraft weapons. The major difference between escorting Stukas and escorting bombers was that the Stuka had to be protected during the dive and re-assembly after pull out. The escort cover that usually arrived at the pull out altitude shortly before the Stukas got there normally did this. The pull out altitude had to be established in advance in the mission field orders because that was the moment when the attackers were the most vulnerable. When there was any modification of plans during the mission all units had to be notified by radio so the changes could be coordinated. It was simply not possible for the fighters to protect each individual Stuka, so the Ju 87 pilots tried to keep a formation of three aircraft while closing up with others as quickly as possible after a dive. When the weather was marginal and the Stukas had to dive through a cloud formation, it was impossible to keep any sort of a position in relation to others, so they always suffered heavy losses because there was no way to exercise good coordination.

The greatest drawback to successful Stuka bombing was the very limited speed of 155 MPH in level flight. During the Battle of Britain these aircraft were usually operated around 16,000 feet and in Russia at about 6,500 feet and this would put all aircraft directly into the range of medium and heavy flak. The minimum pull out altitude was 1,900 feet so the Stukas almost always flew right on down to the ground after their bombing dives and they then would attack tanks and other mobile equipment on the way home.

Any rendezvous with a fighter escort had to be programmed with great care because the Stuka was so slow and vulnerable. In Africa where enemy fighters almost never appeared behind the German lines, the Stukas would fly over fighter bases at 6,000 feet at a predetermined time. Fighter pilots would already be in their cockpits so when the Stukas appeared they would start their engines. The Stukas would then fly on to the front as the fighters caught up to them before they arrived at the target. Thus, a rendezvous was always assured and the fighters could conserve fuel. However, this type of rendezvous could be successful only as long as the German held air superiority.

At the target a number of escort fighters actually dove with the Stukas or fighter-bombers or ground attack aircraft in order to cover them at their most vulnerable moment, even pulling out of the dive with them. This was very difficult to do because the fighters had greater diving speed and were forced to weave to slow down during this part of the attack.

Radio silence was always mandatory, especially if enemy formations or even friendly formations were sighted because it was always possible that a false report that the enemy was present would cause the pilots of the bomb carrying aircraft to jettison their bombs unnecessarily. To keep this from happening, only the most experienced pilots and formation leaders were allowed to broadcast the presence of enemy aircraft. When strikes involved tank destroying Stukas the Germans found it necessary to have the fighter escort shoot up enemy anti-aircraft installations in the vicinity of the target to reduce the danger to the slower attacking aircraft.

Since Hitler had been so greatly influenced by pre-war concepts, leading him to believe dive-bombing was the most accurate form of attack from the air. Göring hesitated to disagree with him. German light bombers like the Ju 88 and the Do 217 and heavy bombers such as the He 177 had to be able to make this kind of attack. As a result these aircraft when so equipped, performed so poorly that they could seldom be used to conduct either daytime level bombing or dive bombing missions. The job of escorting any of these aircraft was always magnified during dive bombing strikes because the defensive armament was so ineffective. In addition, the limited maneuverability of the Ju 88 during dive and pull out resulted in a wide spread formation and re-assembly took even more time than the Stukas, so losses were ridiculously high. During the Battle of Britain the Ju 88 had to be taken off dive bombing strikes and was only used for high altitude level bombing. Still, the *Luftwaffe* High Command insisted right up to the end of the war that all tactical aircraft had to be equipped to carry bombs and that the pilots had to be trained in dive bombing techniques even though this kind of strike was not used by multi-engine aircraft.

As a result of *Luftwaffe* experiences in Spain and in Poland, no fighter escort was found to be necessary for ground attack aircraft during the French campaign in 1940. Fighters were regularly sent to sweep the combat area clear of enemy aircraft so ground attack formations could deliver their bombs unmolested. At the time, only one ground attack Group, attached to Richthofen's Tactical Air Force, *Fliegerkorps* VIII, was in existence to do this job. This unit was initially equipped with the Henschel 123 biplane, but after the campaign in the West these obsolete aircraft were replaced by the Bf 109 fighter-bombers. This unit later flew during the Battle of Britain but only as a level bombing group and even then they had to have fighter escort cover because of strong RAF retaliation.

In 1941 when the campaign in Russia began, the *Luftwaffe* had a single attack Group consisting of three Squadrons of Bf 109s and one Squadron of Henschel 123s. In early 1942, two more ground attack units equipped with Bf 109s and Bf 110s were added. This increase brought about a corresponding increase in the requirement for fighter cover though they tried to provide their own whenever possible. Often when there was an Army break through on the ground, the Germans would schedule concentrated missions in which twin-engine bombers, Stukas, and ground attack units all attacked one after another on a given target. These mass strikes were usually covered by an air umbrella of all available fighter aircraft except those that were required for close escort of the bombers and Stukas. Several squadrons of Henschel-129s equipped with large caliber cannons would also be used as tank destroyers. All these aircraft were attached to fighter wings in order to provide a strike force with heavy firepower should the Russians break through the front lines at any time. In the summer of 1943, the *Luftwaffe* concentrated all these units operationally. The fighter groups were subordinated to the tank destroyer units and the proper coordination resulted by using the tank destroyers en masse. This turned out to be quite successful.

Also in 1943, all ground attack aircraft including the Ju 87s were replaced by the Fw 190. After this conversion, there was no longer any need for fighter cover except in special cases. The *Luftwaffe* still insisted on using sweeps by the regular fighter forces to clear the battle area prior to any strike by ground attack units even though the number of fighters available became more and more limited. However, the limited number of Stukas that were still left on operations required regular fighter escort right up to the end of the war.

In Africa there were two ground attack Groups equipped with Fw 190s which always made strikes with a ratio of one escorting fighter for each one actually delivering bombs. As the Allies gradually gained air superiority over Tunis, Sicily and Italy, they were moved accordingly, but they always experienced great difficulties because their losses became so high. There was also one tank destroyer Squadron in the Southern Theater, but it eventually was not able to operate with any effectiveness and was finally transferred to the Russian front for obvious reasons.

Just one ground attack unit was available when the Allies invaded Europe and it could only be launched when provided with a very strong escort. The Allied fighter umbrella hovered almost continuously over many of the *Luftwaffe* fighter bases so it became virtually impossible for the Fighter Force to get airborne in any large numbers because any assembly or rendezvous was either broken up in the air or prohibited from taking off in the first place. With such oppressive air superiority there was almost no opportunity to get any sort of planned mission off the ground either. On the 1st of January 1945, the *Luftwaffe* was able to mount a successful surprise "Big Blow" strike, but this last really large effort came off only because of the personal leadership and initiative of the formation leaders. With the combination of air superiority, good fighting spirit, well trained pilots, excellent radar and operational control, the Allies were successful in disrupting every German air effort almost immediately.

Although the *Luftwaffe* had used fighter bombers throughout the campaigns in Poland and France, they did not use this type of attack against England until the fall of 1940. When this decision was made, many units that became involved in dive-bombing had not mastered the art of aerial combat as it was developing, and so they were inexperienced in the changing requirements of aerial warfare. As a result it became mandatory to hold many conferences with bomber, fighter-bomber and escort squadron commanders in order to clarify and refine the operational tactics that were evolving. Every time the German Air Force tried a new innovation, the RAF defenders retaliated with a counter innovation, and so another change in tactics would then be necessary.

Initially, on most missions, the fighter-bombers flew together in a closer formation than the fighter escort that was usually positioned to the right, left, or high rear. In the course of the battle, the RAF always tried to concentrate on the fighter-bombers, so the *Luftwaffe* adopted the tactic of mixing bomb carrying aircraft in between pure fighters because it was hard to tell the difference from a distance since all Bf 109's looked alike. The fighter-bombers concentrated on area targets such as London. City, harbors, oil depots, and airfields while attacking from high altitude after a shallow, diving approach from about 23,000 feet. Smaller targets had to be attacked from lower altitude. Speed was always increased by making a long shallow dive that began a great distance out from the target. Since it was very difficult for the bombers and fighters to maintain a close formation, the problems of escort were quite complicated. After bomb release the fighter-bombers used their speed to get away from the target area and the escort fighters were released to pursue RAF fighters at will.

Since the *Luftwaffe* leaders considered the losses of fighter-bombers to be acceptable during the Battle of Britain, the High Command demanded that more and more fighter bombers be employed even though there had never been any training programs for this type of mission. Fighter units merely installed bomb racks, put on bombs and then went off on sorties. At this time Wings were conducting purely fighter missions against England and they had no real interest in dropping bombs. At the time, the *Luftwaffe* was launching two and often three strikes across the Channel each day when the weather permitted.

When orders were received to convert a Wing to fighter-bombers, only one third of the aircraft were re-equipped. Wings were at liberty to carry out the conversion in several ways either by converting one whole Group to fighter bombing or by converting one Squadron in each of the three groups. The latter solution seemed to work better because small fighter-bomber formations needed less escort cover. Each of the fighter Groups considered themselves to be pure fighters, so the bombs were carried as inconspicuously as possible. All of this became a disadvantage because special ground handling equipment was required on three bases instead of just one.

By late fall of 1941 in the campaign against England, the *Luftwaffe* was forced by bad weather to cease fighter-bomber operations even though a few feeble attempts were still made to drop bombs without seeing the ground. During the winter some fighter-bomber strikes were scheduled against shipping, but these were generally unsuccessful because the pilots had never received training for this kind of complicated attack. However, in the spring of 1942, the *Luftwaffe* began to conduct surprise attacks against shipping in Squadron strength and actually achieved some success. To avoid English radar, the aircraft flew at sea level just a few feet above the waves while maintaining absolute radio silence. Enemy aircraft were frequently encountered when the RAF established a fighter patrol over a convoy or conducted an area patrol in an effort to blockade this kind of sneak German attack.

Eventually, these successful shipping strikes convinced Hitler to order revenge and retaliation raids. These raids were directed at English historical and artistic monuments that were listed in the German Biedecker Directory for Tourists, so the RAF referred to them as the "Biedecker Raids." Again, the success of these strikes depended on surprise and deception and concise planning was required because usually over one hundred dive-bombers were sent out en masse. These strikes always approached the English coast at very low altitude then climbed to medium altitude for the actual attack. After bombs had been released, the retiring fighters hit the deck for the return to home base. Usually, a small close escort force accompanied the fighter-bombers to the target while a much larger formation of straight fighters tried to engage the RAF at higher altitudes while the strike was in progress. In every case, the Germans got to their targets successfully, but they were usually cut off on the return flight by RAF fighter blockade patrols which made them battle their way out. This tactic always caused very heavy losses because the Bf 109s were prevented from heading on a direct line for home, and they frequently ran out of fuel. Still more fighter-bombers were lost to anti-aircraft fire than were lost to RAF fighter pilots.

The fighter forces were often called upon to escort ship convoys and naval units since the Germans did not have aircraft carriers or carrier type aircraft. In the early stages of the conquest of Europe there was no necessity to provide escort for ships at sea because all the battles were on the ground. However, the invasion of Norway made shipping escort mandatory, so a Corps was established to carry out the necessary air operations. One *Zerstörer* Wing equipped with Bf 110s and a fighter wing with Bf 109s were located at Schleswig-Holstein in the beginning of the campaign, and later transferred to Aalborg and several fields in North Jutland. The Germans rapidly found out that the range of the Bf 110 was inadequate to perform the tasks assigned and it became necessary to add external fuel tanks. It also became necessary to establish regulations for this kind of undertaking since there was no previous experience to rely upon. In general, this type of mission was successful because the British usually made attacks on shipping with antiquated Blenheim bombers and obsolete torpedo aircraft which were easily shot down by the German fighter escort.

Beginning in 1940, the Navy made greater demands for fighter cover for small coastal convoys, individual ships, and especially for tankers all along the French Coast. After Autumn, 1941, ships could only move during darkness at night while laying over during the day in ports because there were just not enough fighters to provide escort except only for the most pressing requirements. Usually, the Navy gave Fighter Command the times and locations of ships when asking for specific fighter cover to insure that it would be ready when needed. However, no attempt was made to provide each Navy unit with continuous fighter escort, and fighters would only scramble when the Listening Service or radar plots indicated that enemy action was pending.

In late Autumn of 1940, Hitler's military machine began preparations for "Operation Sea Lion" which was to be the invasion of Great Britain, but these efforts were not taken seriously by the *Luftwaffe*. General Galland's Wing, JG 26 was supposed to be the first to transfer to England, a singular if somewhat dubious honor. Loading plans were developed and the Germans went so far as to practice loading and landing maneuvers up and down the Belgian and Dutch Coasts on a small scale. However, by the middle of 1942, the English had established air superiority over the Channel so it was virtually impossible to conduct any kind of sea transport without interference. Limited convoys were attempted occasionally provided fighter cover was available. By this time, the German Navy was enthralled with the "Blockade Runner" concept and great attention was devoted to escorting single vessels in and out of ports. When it was necessary to provide escort for great distances out to sea it was accomplished by a *Zerstörer* Wing with two Groups of Ju 88s and one Group of Me 410s supplemented by a Squadron of Arado 196s, all based in Brittany. These units were always attacked by British Mosquito's and other bomber and torpedo aircraft as well as long ranged American fighters and it was necessary to escort all aircraft returning from heavy combat by a Group of Fw 190s carrying external fuel tanks. Much of the time the escorting fighters suffered heavy losses from the RAF.

When the Russian campaign began in the Summer of 1941, and the Germans were forced to move all but two fighter wings to the East for obvious reasons, the Allies began to make ship movements at night in bad weather with ships equipped with a great variety of anti-aircraft weaponry. The fighter units tried as best they could to provide cover for the German motor torpedo boats called *Schnellbooten* which were about the only surface vessels the Navy could use in the English Channel. The young and daring *Schnellbooten* Flotilla leaders had much in common with the Commanders of the fighter forces and they conferred so frequently that mutual understanding was maintained. The German fighter escort usually escorted at low altitude, gaining height to begin combat with the

RAF when fighters and fighter-bombers appeared. After each engagement, there was always a conference between Fleet Commanders and the *Luftwaffe* C.O.'s to review the outcome and to correct mistakes for the future.

The *Luftwaffe* Flying Commander, Atlantic was also required to provide escort for U-boat fleets. Since the enemy tried to disrupt any U-boat traffic with depth charges, bombs and cannon it was necessary for the Air Force to protect larger formations of U-boats from these low level attacks. As time went by, these missions became more and more difficult because of the ever increasing technical performance of the enemy aircraft, overwhelming air superiority and the development of excellent Allied radar. Although there was good coordination between the U-boat Commanders and the airmen, losses were high in both single-engine and twin-engine fighter units so that the escort almost took on the appearance of suicide missions. The pilots believed it was necessary to protect the U-boats at all costs because there were so many lives at stake in each individual submarine crew, not to mention the effect each boat could have on the outcome of the war.

The Germans astounded the world when they successfully moved the warships *Prinz Eugen*, *Scharnhorst*, and *Gneisenau* from Brest to the North Sea. Hitler directed Galland to personally prepare and conduct this operation in order to make the transfer possible. The Navy demanded that the *Luftwaffe* provide enough air cover to make this great fleet secure from all enemy air attacks, so the preparations had to be made with the utmost secrecy and deception if the mission was to be successful. Since this was the first really large scale joint effort between the Navy and the Air Force, detailed planning was absolutely necessary because, relatively speaking, only a few fighter aircraft were available. A detailed and exhaustive "Memorandum for the Conduct of Fighter Escort for Sea Forces and Large Naval Forces" was prepared and circulated to all units that were to be involved.

The fighter effort was organized into close escort against low level attacks from medium altitudes, and a blockade patrol was conducted some distance away from the convoy. In addition the plan called for protection against any kind of aerial action such as high level dive bombing attacks or fighter sweeps by the enemy. During the entire period of action there were only 40 to 50 fighter aircraft available, but still there had to be an over-lap of 15 to 20 minutes as one patrol relieved another. Reserve forces in group strength were held in readiness to be scrambled in case of really heavy enemy attacks and a control station was set up on one of the vessels involved to coordinate the fighters and anti-aircraft weaponry.

Galland operated from a command post in a special Ju 52 transport that was equipped with elaborate communications gear he could use to control ground operations. Night fighters operating as twin-engine day fighters turned out to be especially effective because of their all weather capability. As the convoy proceeded along the North Sea Coast all aircraft were transferred from base to base along with the fighter control center in the air. In Norway, control was turned over to the *Jafu*, Norwegian who had his own fighter forces take over cover responsibility from Trondheim until the final destination was reached. After the ships reached their destination, the High Command acknowledged that the success of the entire operation was due for the most part to the *Luftwaffe*. However, as a contributing factor, the attacking RAF aircraft always flew without fighter cover so the unusually small force of German fighters were able to achieve astonishing success. In preparation for the future the *Luftwaffe* made minor changes in doctrine, but a major mission of this nature was never undertaken again.

When the *Luftwaffe* began to provide escort for shipping in the Mediterranean, the English countered with greatly increased air activity. The Allies had such superior forces that the demands made by both the German and Italian navies for aerial protection would have required more fighter wings than existed in the entire theater. In addition, the Italian Navy ignored instructions in combat orders and they paid no attention to accurate timing, composition of forces or routes to be sailed so it was virtually impossible to provide them with any kind of air support. Even though Italian fighter wings participated in shipping escort they were only able to contribute a small number of aircraft and when they did the pilots were undependable. As a result the *Luftwaffe* failed to meet all the necessary demands by a wide margin.

Supply routes in Africa were so long that continuous escort for shipping could only be provided by such limited numbers of aircraft that they could not be effective against the powerful strikes the enemy directed at convoys or even individual ships. As the battle in Africa reached a crisis and all fighter forces were assigned to protect shipping but the *Luftwaffe* was still unable to provide adequate protection. The Allies had such over-whelming air superiority that even scramble take-offs were unsuccessful because long ranged Allied fighters defeated the *Luftwaffe* in every single battle. When the Germans tried to evacuate their ground forces by air the *Luftwaffe* transport aircraft met with disaster and were almost completely destroyed because they were very, very slow and could never have been adequately escorted by fighters even if they had been faster.

Although Anglo-American air superiority made any air-sea rescue extremely hazardous, this activity was an absolute necessity to keep the morale of the fighter pilot high. The service was most effective in areas where Allied fighter aircraft were not able to operate for obvious reasons. Escort fighters were used to locate any known sea crashes, maintain contact over the downed airmen, and then lead the sea rescue boats to the scene. Escort was always provided, not because the enemy might strafe the downed airman in the water but because the Allies would often attempt to effect a rescue in order to capture a prisoner and thus gain valuable intelligence information. Because of this, friendly fighters provided cover on the approach, during rescue, and all the way back to friendly territory.

The whole history of the *Luftwaffe* Fighter Arm is a clear demonstration of misapplication of capability. General Galland expressed in one brief paragraph what has been detailed in this entire chapter of fighters up by his following sentiments: "The fighter pilot's element is to attack, to track, to hunt, and to destroy the enemy. Only in this way can the eager and skillful fighter pilot display his ability to the fullest. Tie him to a narrow and confined task, rob him of his initiative and you take away from him the best and most valuable qualities he possesses: aggressive spirit, joy of action, and the passion of the hunter. The fighter arm cannot be manacled particularly when its fetters are undermined by earthbound thinking. By its intrinsic properties the fighter arm belongs to the elite. The almost unbelievably expensive product of clever designers, precise technicians, and specialized workers, given into the hands of scientifically chosen and comprehensively trained experts constitutes an arm of the highest efficiency, but also one of great delicacy. It can be compared with a razor blade that must be guided by a sensitive hand. The man who uses it like a hatchet must not be surprised if it turns jagged in his hand and finally becomes useless."

CHAPTER TEN

Army Air Support

Because there was very little knowledge or experience existing any-where in the world which the Germans could use to advantage when they decided to rebuild the *Luftwaffe*, they were forced to develop their own operational philosophies. No doubt some of the lessons they learned during the campaign in Spain were useful, but Hitler considered the primary role of the *Luftwaffe* was to support the Army on the ground and events in Poland and the Low Countries justified his contention. His interference in the principles of operation and the desire to please him on the part of the high level *Luftwaffe* staff influenced GAF planners to adopt guidelines which made it necessary for Air Force units to support the Army in combat in every possible way.

From the beginning, the Germans realized it would be necessary to achieve air superiority if Army support operations were to be conducted successfully. If it was not possible to establish continuous air superiority, at the very least, local superiority had to be assured by the fighter forces during an actual attack. *Luftwaffe* experience in Spain and elsewhere clearly demonstrated that excellent communications facilities were absolutely demanded in order to provide quick and close cooperation with the Army. Also, it was mandatory to have the Air Force and the Army Listening Services providing rapid evaluations of the tactical ground situation based on what was heard from the enemy communications. In developing ground support procedures they found that the Army and Air Force had to use the same maps with the same scales at all levels of command and wherever possible, photographic maps with appropriate grid designations of important ground features were a must.

As a basic rule, the Air Force would only be directed to attack targets that the Army could not destroy by using its own medium and heavy combat weapons. It was policy that the Army had to establish a priority list of support requirements, eliminating any operations that were not absolutely necessary. In the final analysis, it was up to the *Luftwaffe* to decide if, when, and where any attacks would be made. Experience dictated that once an attack was decided upon, it had to be delivered with enough force to achieve certain success. Any operation conducted with a weak force was a total waste because it would not be successful and probably would not even improve the morale of the soldiers on the ground. This was a lesson that the United States certainly should have taken advantage of during the entire war in Vietnam.

It was of utmost importance to maintain continuous air surveillance of the tactical battle area because pilots attacking targets on the ground had to be provided with enough target information to make these attacks successful. If this was not possible, the Army Air Support Arm of the *Luftwaffe* became only a sort of mobile long ranged field artillery which could only attack targets that had been discovered by reconnaissance on the ground. If this were the case, then there would be no way to exploit the wide range of capabilities of a ground fighter force. The Germans found out early on in the war that airfields used by Army ground support units had to be close to the front lines because of the limited range of the aircraft which allowed for penetration of only about 150km into enemy territory. Naturally, they could direct more missions at the enemy when the flights were short because it would not be necessary to carry large quantities of fuel. The closer the aircraft were to the Army, the easier it was to provide adequate communications between command elements of both the Army and the Air Force, because the lines were shorter and therefore more dependable. Every time the Army advanced, it was necessary to provide emergency landing fields as quickly as possible, and it was also necessary to have anti-aircraft protection in place around those fields to prevent enemy strategic attacks when the friendly aircraft were transferred to these new locations. Logistical support for the advanced units such as ammunition, bombs, and bomb containers had to be moved forward ahead of time so that aircraft could be prepared for quick turn around to launch additional strikes as soon as they had landed at the new location at the end of a transfer mission.

Day Army Air Support Wings were organized into three Groups of three Squadrons, each equipped with 12 aircraft. The Germans often considered enlarging each Squadron to 16 aircraft and pilots without enlarging the group headquarters in order to achieve a better utilization of men and equipment as well as increasing operational readiness. They knew that weak formations were unable to achieve success in the face of strong enemy formations and defenses. Large friendly formations would be able to fight longer and much more effectively. They did not go to larger and larger formations though because it would have been impossible to make quick turn around after each mission and the take-off's and landings of any larger formations would have taken up too much time. German fighters had such limited duration of flight anyway that the problems associated with landing and take off would have reduced penetration range even more than was necessary. The Wing and Group Staffs had six ground attack aircraft attached as headquarters flights so each could provide a combat capability without taking pilots away from any of the Squadrons.

The Germans differentiated between ground attack aircraft and anti-tank ground attack aircraft because each was differently equipped. Pilots were especially trained to perform each of these tasks separately because they each required different tactics and techniques. Although both were considered to operate in support of the Army on the ground, they were specially designated and operated apart from each other. However, they would perform together operationally when the occasion demanded.

Special anti-tank ground attack units in Russia were usually equipped with 16 to 20 aircraft and pilots. Each Wing had an additional Squadron that could be used to augment this strength for any especially heavy efforts. The anti-tank units were usually committed in Squadron strength at the Russian Front, and they seldom operated altogether as a Group. The Germans found out early in the Russian campaign that it was necessary to assign 16 aircraft to each Squadron in order to make even half way effective attacks on the enemy tank forces, so the organization of all ground attack anti-tank units was constant right up to the end of the war. In all anti-tank units it was an established policy that parts of each Squadron would carry bombs to suppress enemy anti-aircraft defenses during a raid. In this manner anti-tank pilots would not have to rely on rendezvous or simultaneous operations with other regular ground attack units.

Night ground attack Squadrons on the Russian Front had 20 aircraft and there were either two or three Squadrons in a Group. Since there were no effective night fighter defenses on the Eastern Front, all aircraft in commission were used for every mission. With proper operational procedures, there was no problem with landings and takeoffs in spite of the large numbers of aircraft involved because the enemy was unable to counter attack from the air at night. Since there was little need for dispersal, several Squadrons of each Group could be located on the same airfield thus simplifying communications. However, the quality and performance of night fighter pilots was never up to a high standard even though efforts were made to achieve improvement right up to the end of the war.

Pilots selected for day ground attack operations were generally adequately qualified because those who were not entirely suitable were eliminated in flying schools or in operational training units before they actually got into combat. The *Luftwaffe* usually assigned officers with previous ground attack experience to command the primary flying schools so they could then participate in the selection of men to be assigned to the ground attack forces. With skilled instruction, good pilots could be taught to enjoy ground attack missions and they would often volunteer for these assignments. However, there were never enough new pilots to fulfill the vacancies in the ground attack forces because there were only limited numbers of recruits entering the flying schools, so pilots were solicited from other branches of the *Luftwaffe*. Often pilots who had been relieved from duty with other branches were made available, but those who had been relieved because they were unsuitable failed just as badly in the ground attack arm. Pilots who were relieved from flying operations because they had difficulty flying at high altitude, but were capable otherwise often became excellent at ground attack work because the missions were always performed at lower altitudes.

Surplus pilots were continually being made available by reductions in reconnaissance units, but the ground attack forces accepted only those who had single-engine experience. These pilots usually proved to be excellent for ground attack work because they understood the requirement for air-ground support for the Army as a result of their reconnaissance experience. Bomber pilots were not good at this kind of mission because it was very difficult for them to convert to single-engine aircraft after flying multi-engine bombers. Besides, they usually had difficulty maintaining position in large maneuvering formations. Surprisingly, bomber pilots always had good operational morale, a great willingness, and a stubborn determination to complete any mission regardless of losses. Usually, these men were shot down the very first time they were sent into combat on ground attack missions.

Pilots who had been relieved from transport or liaison units were usually sent to night ground attack units as long as they had what was considered to be good character. There were always enough of them available so that a careful selection could be made. However, when units converted from the Ju 87 that was ponderous and slow, to the Fw 190, many pilots could not cope with the increased speed and performance characteristics. Still, many did become good ground attack pilots at night. Old instructors from primary schools proved to be very good at night ground attack also even though they were too old to be used for day fighter or day ground attack work. The Fw 190 night ground attack pilots had to be exceptionally well trained in addition to possessing excellent character. Fully capable replacements were very difficult to find because pilots who had a special knack for gunnery usually liked to attack tanks. Generally, they were always assigned to the anti-tank units because this mission had very high priority.

Flight Leaders in ground attack units had to be very capable at flying in formation, they had to be able to grasp the entire battle area situation at a glance, and they had to be able to recognize targets on the ground and in the air almost instantly. Squadron Commanders were appointed only after they had enough combat experience to be considered highly qualified. Often young officers were promoted to Squadron Commander while older officers in the Group remained as ordinary pilots or flight leaders. Group and Wing Commanders were usually officers who had successful records as commanders in lower levels such as Squadrons or Groups. In ground attack forces, A Squadron or Group Commander who was in line for promotion was taken off combat operations for a period of six months to one year. He would act as a Group or Wing Commander in a training organization where he had the opportunity to become acquainted with his new responsibilities. Later, when he took over command of an operational unit, he would then have the administrative knowledge required for his new position. In addition, he would be able to rest up for the new tour of duty at the same time he was using his operational experience to teach new pilots going through the training organization. This process was not always successful because there was a great shortage of officers who were qualified for command positions. Officers who were no longer qualified for operational assignments were sent to pilot and officer training schools so they could continue to influence the assignment of good men to the ground attack arm.

At the beginning of the war, technical officers were flying officers who had been given special technical training. Since it was necessary for every formation leader to have some knowledge of technical matters, a logical path to promotion was to take technical courses and gain experience as a technical officer. Naturally, technical officers wanted to fly on operational missions so most of them flew too much and worried too little about their primary responsibilities. As the supply of good officers gradually dried up, it became impossible to assign them exclusively to non-flying responsibilities regardless of how much training they had received, so the *Luftwaffe* was forced to use older chief mechanics and grounded officer pilots as technical officers. The latter became quite capable once they had completed the required technical schools. When this policy was implemented, the units often achieved a commission rate of over 70% this was considered to be excellent in any air force.

Maintenance organizations were almost the same in all fighter units. There were enough maintenance people to enable a unit to send an advance team to prepare a new airfield. These teams called "Werkommandos" assisted maintenance crews who arrived with the aircraft at new bases, so continued operational missions could be carried out. Ground support equipment was held to a minimum just as it was in all fighter units. Since ground attack units always operated at low altitudes there was no need for oxygen equipment, but, on the other hand, it was necessary to augment the bomb loading equipment on hand. At all times the *Luftwaffe* tried to make the ground attack units independent of any additional ground support personnel or equipment. Fighter Commanders found out early on that both the Fw 190 and the Bf 109 were capable of carrying mechanics in the fuselage behind the pilot and several mechanics would be transported in this manner each time a unit moved from one base to another. Of course, if the fighter was involved in aerial combat and shot down, the entire crew on board would perish along with the pilot.

As to weaponry, small fragmentation bombs in containers were found to be the most effective against ground troops in open country or in positions which offered no protection against air attacks. This was because of the carpeting effect they produced. Proximity fuses which caused the bombs to explode above the ground were considered to be less effective than impact fuses. The same bombs were used against enemy personnel and operating heavy weapons providing they were in the open. Strafing attacks were effective against personnel and lighter weapons, but had no effect against heavy equipment. The Germans did attempt to destroy armored trains and railroad guns with larger and heavier bombs.

The *Luftwaffe* had very little success in destroying concrete bridges because it required a direct hit with a heavy bomb, but once in a while a lucky hit would bring down a span. Even so, traffic was usually only temporarily halted. If it was not possible to bomb the enemy as they made repairs, it was always easy for them to erect pontoon bridges. However, the Germans quickly came to the conclusion that, under certain tactical situations when the enemy was being pursued through escape routes leading out of surrounded areas or when there were threats and forward movements of reserve forces, it was imperative to bomb bridges. These attacks had to be made regardless of whether or not they were expected to be successful.

The *Luftwaffe* considered attacks on enemy airfields to be a part of Army support, so they usually concentrated on dispersed aircraft by making attacks with fragmentation bombs. Early in the war, the GAF discovered it was not worth while to attack fixed installations like hangers because the enemy usually dispersed his aircraft. The Germans felt that railroad lines were worthwhile targets, especially when the enemy was bringing troops to the front or taking them away from a specific battle area. It was always desirable to cut tracks leading into or out of stations, or to block bridges or valleys, but it was useless to bomb open stretches of track since repair was so simple. Trains in motion could often be wrecked with heavy bombs and then the troops streaming from them could be attacked with fragmentation bombs and machine gun fire. The Germans always made a special effort to destroy locomotives, especially when there were little or no repair facilities located in the vicinity. Rockets and cannon were especially effective, but smaller weapons only caused slight damage. However, even this would often help if the attacks were made in remote areas.

Whenever the Army was on the defensive, the *Luftwaffe* ground attack units made concentrated efforts to attack the enemy assembly areas. These attacks could be very effective if the enemy made tank attacks or used artillery or reserve troops in the action. In these cases the *Luftwaffe* would launch attacks both day and night to rob the enemy of his momentum. Naturally, when there was an enemy tank break through the anti-tank aircraft and the ground attack aircraft operated in unison because it was often impossible to spot obscure positions from the air. The ground attack pilots could only gain an advantage when the enemy ran into a choke point such as a river or a bridge crossing. The Germans tried to develop a procedure to use radio control so that ground attack aircraft could make attacks in bad weather but the lead time to develop the equipment was so great that this method could only have been perfected long after the war had ended.

Ground attacks could be carried out in Group, Squadron, Flight or element strength and were conducted in Wing strength only in exceptional cases when huge ground forces were involved. When the war started in 1937, seven Groups had Fw 190s and fifteen were equipped with the Stuka, but, by the end of the war, all but one Ju 87 unit had converted to the Fw 190 for obvious reasons. Experience taught the Germans that when the enemy had both anti-aircraft weapons and defensive fighter aircraft any ground attacks would be very difficult, especially in Italy and the Western Front. In fact, it was virtually impossible to conduct any strikes at all if the *Luftwaffe* did not have at least local air superiority over the battle area at the time. If they did not, the aircraft losses were too high in relation to what was actually accomplished against the enemy because pilots had to be able to carry out their attacks without fear of enemy fighters if they were to achieve any accuracy at all. If there was no enemy fighter opposition, attacking forces could make individual attacks in a wide-open dispersed manner. However, they had to maintain a tightly closed up formation for protection when enemy aircraft were present. On the Eastern Front it was usually possible for part of the attacking formation to provide escort for the others at the beginning of the attack just by remaining at high altitude. When the first attackers had dropped their bombs, they then provided top cover while the rest of the force attacked. If enemy aircraft arrived on the scene, it was necessary to jettison bombs that were always armed whenever GAF fighters flew over enemy territory.

If the enemy had superiority it was always necessary for regular fighter units to provide escort, and strong fighter opposition would always force the fighter bombers to make either concentrated high altitude diving attacks or low level surprise strikes. Under these conditions it was impossible to strafe even though the Fw 190 had both cannon and machine guns. Further, the bombing was always less accurate and therefore much less effective. The ultimate goal of every ground attack mission was to fight the enemy down to the last round of ammunition, to destroy all recognizable targets, and to remain over the battle area as long as possible while making every movement of the enemy impossible so air superiority was a must. Weather had a great influence on the type of mission to be flown as well as the size of formation that could be used and attacks under low ceilings always resulted in higher losses of attack aircraft. The attacking aircraft were too easily sighted by enemy aircraft and anti-aircraft batteries. When silhouetted against the clouds and heavy losses were the result.

Whenever the enemy made a lucky tank break through, the Army was usually not in a position to throw enough of its own tanks or anti-aircraft weapons against the thrust to stop it, so the *Luftwaffe* always had to come to the rescue. In the spring and autumn in Russia, the roads were so bad and the ground so muddy it was almost impossible to bring tanks into position to retaliate and the only possibility to reverse an attack was to use the special anti-tank Stuka attack units. The Germans found out the hard way that ground attack aircraft were not able to destroy enough tanks with ordinary cannon, machine guns and bombs, but the special anti-tank aircraft were very successful with their armor piercing cannon and special anti-tank rockets. The Henschel 129, the Ju 87, and the Fw 190 were all used with great success when rocket tubes were attached to the bomb racks. It was always a big mistake to make attacks against tank assembly areas. The enemy always surrounded them with a large number of antiaircraft weapons and the attackers suffered very heavy losses. As a counter, the Germans learned to attack with large formations of aircraft carrying a great number of containers of hollow charge armor piercing bombs which were dropped from high altitude some distance away, outside the range of anti-aircraft fire.

When enemy tanks actually broke through into friendly troop areas, the Germans had to use only the special anti-tank units because they could attack with enough accuracy to avoid endangering the friendly forces. At the same time, the normal ground attack pilots would attack lightly armored support vehicles that normally followed the tanks. However, the Russians usually supported each tank breakthrough with strong fighter cover in good weather, so it was necessary to drive off the top cover as a prerequisite to making successful attacks with anti-tank aircraft. Bad weather was ideal for the antitank pilots because they usually attacked at low altitudes anyway, so they were able to operate best underneath cloud cover.

It was always necessary to suppress enemy anti-aircraft defenses in order to make a successful anti-tank attack. So, after the Germans had conducted a long series of successful strikes against Russian tanks, the enemy began to increase heavy anti-aircraft protection for all his mobile vehicles right up to the end of the war. By that time almost every nation had some sort of anti-aircraft tank which could protect other tanks. The Germans had to make attacks in the shortest possible time to counter this developing capability and to achieve the element of surprise while attempting to keep the enemy from unlimbering his guns in preparation to fire. This kind of an attack required an experienced pilot with extensive practice in tank recognition because it was necessary to destroy a tank on the first pass in order to be successful without heavy losses. In the last years of the war, the Russians became accustomed to anti-tank attacks and would camouflage their machines whenever possible. As soon as they were aware of approaching *Luftwaffe* anti-tank aircraft, they sought cover near houses, tree clumps or hay stacks. The tanks could only be located by the tracks they made in the dirt, but the Russians usually erased these tracks by dragging heavy tree branches behind their tanks.

The anti-tank aircraft usually fought in elements, flights, and Squadron sizes. When larger units arrived over the battlefield at the same time, the Germans found there would be much confusion and the aircraft usually got in each other's way. Since the most effective range was about one hundred to one hundred and fifty yards, the firing run made by each pilot had to be very steady and this required great concentration and personal determination. Good intelligence regarding the disposition of enemy defensive firepower was absolutely necessary because heavy weapons fire would naturally distract the attention of the attackers.

The Germans used night ground attack aircraft to harass the enemy in both the front and rear areas exactly as the day ground attack units did. They actually stole this idea from the Russians initially by using training aircraft to carry out these raids. However, by the end of 1943, when German ground attack units were unable to operate in the daytime without great difficulty because of Allied air superiority, they began to use Stukas at night quite successfully, especially against the Anzio beach head. As a result, all night ground attack units were soon converted to the Stuka or the Fw 190. When sufficient numbers were available, these aircraft would continually harass the enemy all night by hindering night marches, holding down artillery fire, and turning back night-attacks. Night ground attack missions had to be directed against broad areas because it was impossible to pin point targets at night. Firing artillery, lighted transport columns, bridges, villages, and troop concentrations all proved to be excellent targets. Illuminated targets were best and dark targets had to be illuminated with flares dropped from the air or shot from the ground by artillery. Rolling attacks in successive waves each one further forward than the other were usually made all night on the Russian Front. This type of action greatly hindered any preparations the enemy would or could make for counter attacks the following day.

The Germans recognized that it was an absolute necessity to have excellent communications if adequate ground support was to be provided from the air. Telephone equipment had to be available so each unit would have a telephone network connecting all operations centers, dispersal areas, dwellings, and radio stations. In addition, the units often improvised radio telephones between the headquarters and dispersal areas because there were no wires that could be damaged by enemy attacks. Each time a new airfield was established, radio telephones were used until ground wires could be laid down. Teletype machines wore available for Wing Headquarters only, but independently operating Groups would often be authorized to have teletype capability.

Externally, Wing Staffs were linked to the radio network of the next highest headquarters as well as to their own subordinate units, so the

Groups eventually became radio equipped, thus completing the entire communications system. At the end of the war all ground attack units were equipped with the GAF/VHF radio telephone transmitter receiver systems. Some of the night ground attack units were also equipped with ground radio beacons used for locating targets during attacks, and this technique proved to be very successful.

The ground attack units were always located closer to the front lines than any other flying units because their aircraft had such limited range and it was mandatory to reduce the time required to fly to and from the target areas. In wars of movement, there were many advances and retreats so transfers from one base to another were frequent occurrences. Often units were transferred by vehicles and sometimes by transport aircraft, so complete mobility of ground personnel and equipment was always assured even though it was often necessary to borrow trucks from other organizations to do the job. All ground support equipment except that of the Motorized Repair Platoon was air transportable and ground attack units had a flying repair platoon that could rapidly be loaded onto a transport aircraft. Usually there was limited air transport available to the various commands, so the flying units were given only enough space to transport key personnel. These movements, lasting for only a few days, often covered long distances, so flying units found it necessary to conduct combat operations with only a few key people. As a result, there were always only a limited number of aircraft in commission.

The *Luftwaffe* made a tremendous number of mistakes in the management and operation of the Ground Attack Arm, just as they did in all other branches. This was forcefully brought into focus in Africa, Italy and on the Western Front when the Germans lost air superiority. In all these areas, the GAF suffered such heavy losses of men and material that they just could not deliver effective support for the Army on the ground. Even if they had been able to increase the number of combat units, they still would not have been successful unless they could have found some way to regain air superiority. In addition to attacks on small individual targets, it became evident that it was also necessary to attack large target areas, but again there were no twin-engine aircraft in the GAF organized to provide this kind of support. Instead, an attempt was made to use bomber units that were originally designated for strategic operations, and they proved to be most ineffective. When these aircraft were taken away in an attempt to accomplish long range bombing in Russia, they were obviously no longer available to provide tactical air support for the Army in any theater of operations.

Reconnaissance Squadrons, which proved to be very effective when they were attached to each Ground Attack Wing, were dissolved in 1942. It then became necessary for each Wing to conduct its own reconnaissance missions. However, the crews did not have adequate training in reconnaissance and diverting tactical aircraft to this type of mission reduced unit ability to make concentrated attacks with great striking power. Despite the ever increasing effectiveness of enemy defenses, the outmoded Ju 87 was not replaced by the Fw 190 until late in the war, and even then, the technical planners made little or no attempt to increase the range of the Fw 190s then being used for ground attack work. The limited range of these aircraft proved to be a tremendous disadvantage in operations where there were a limited number of front line airfields because it was almost impossible to make long range flights from remote air bases to the tactical areas. When the enemy had air superiority he was always able to disrupt take-offs and landings at airfields near the front. Still, the alternative of locating airfields some distance behind the front lines made it impossible for the attacking force to stay over the battlefield area for any length of time. The Germans never did have much success with any form of pierced steel planking, so they had no capacity for quick airfield construction.

The *Luftwaffe* planned to have every ground attack unit equipped with rocket powered anti-tank weaponry, but they never attained this goal because of the delay in making a decision to start the necessary technical development. In the meantime, it was necessary to use a ground to ground Army rocket that required a great amount of special training because it was not a sophisticated weapon. In addition, the shortage of aviation fuel made it impossible to give the pilots the flying training hours to perfect the delivery techniques required for this weapon. Even when the anti-tank pilots did have the necessary training, it actually became a disadvantage because trained pilots could only be used against tanks or other specialized targets. They were often kept on the ground for fear they would be shot down unnecessarily when they could have been used for ordinary ground attack missions. Rockets, bombs, and bomb containers were never developed for use at low altitude, and this was a special disadvantage in

Russia during bad weather because then ground attack pilots were only able to strafe and this kind of an attack had little or no effect on the enemy. Fuel shortages always prevented adequate pilot training, and this situation led to heavy pilot losses, especially amongst the newer pilots. It also resulted in many unsuccessful missions, especially on operations where the enemy had strong defenses. It was virtually impossible to provide any sort of instrument flying training and so many operations conducted in bad weather were especially dangerous. The replacement flow of senior ground attack officers was almost nonexistent, so when a Squadron or Group Commander was lost it was nearly impossible to provide an experienced replacement for him. There were any number of circumstances where non-commissioned officers led Squadrons on operational missions because no officers were available. The whole pipeline from basic flying training up to the command level was inadequate right from the beginning of the war and eventually this situation became impossible as the Germans suffered increasingly heavy losses. In later stages of the war, there was little opportunity to rotate men between the front line areas and the homeland for rest and recuperation, so combat fatigue naturally reduced the over-all effectiveness.

Since operations of the ground attack units were generally directed by commands which were staffed by officers who had little or no combat experience, the missions that resulted were often impractical and, at best, the aircraft were seldom used to full advantage. The *Luftwaffe* tried to get experienced men for command positions, but there was a shortage of officers with any kind of experience up to the highest levels throughout the entire ground attack arm. Courses in which high commanders, their chiefs of staff, and their operations officers would be given a broad perspective of the operational principles of air force units acting in cooperation with the Army were scheduled for early in 1944, but, because of the rapidly changing complex of the war, none were ever implemented. The Army did not understand the principles of air to ground cooperation and often made impossible demands on the Air Force. The *Luftwaffe* frequently made successful raids, but the Army could not take advantage of these attacks because the Army officers lacked the training and know how to follow up.

In the final analysis, the *Luftwaffe* made a grave mistake when ground attack and anti-tank attack organizations were combined under the office of the *General der Schlachtflieger*. Flying units operating in the tactical areas at the front were not immediately affected so the re-organization had no impact where it was to have done the most good. There never was a well-organized technical plan to increase the capability of the ground attack aircraft by adding new and formidable weaponry and even the replacement of the Ju 87 by the Fw 190 came too late to have any great effect on the outcome of the war. The Army and the Air Force never did cooperate fully, and neither force received enough training to prepare their people for actual combat experience. Above all, the lack of trained air leaders was a disaster. The net result was defeat instead of victory.

CHAPTER ELEVEN

Defense

During periods of dire national emergency flashing the code words, "Defense of the *Reich*" shifted control of the fighter forces to *Luftwaffe* Headquarters in Germany proper in order to insure that attacks would be successfully coordinated against the Allied heavy bomber forces. As the intensity of the air battles increased, Defense of the *Reich* became an urgent requirement instead of just code worded instructions for a shift in control as the Allied Forces compressed the circle surrounding Germany. By this time any deployment of fighter units came about by absolute necessity rather than strategic planning, and usually each re-organization or re-location became imperative because of innovative changes on the part of the Allies.

In the beginning of the war this was not the case. During the Polish campaign only about six-fighter groups were stationed in the West for protective purposes, and, even after the declaration of war by France and England, Germany did not develop any long range contingency plan against the possibility of an aerial offensive onslaught from the West. After the Polish campaign, however, all fighter units were moved behind the West Wall into the Ruhr and into Northwestern Germany. The first time the *Luftwaffe* units had any opportunity to develop tactics for defensive warfare occurred when RAF Wellington bombers initially attacked Wilhelmshafen. Until Germany actually began the campaign in the West, the fighters had been assigned only the mission of defense, but from the beginning of the French campaign until 1941, the fighter arm went almost completely on the offensive. When the Germans invaded Russia, most of the fighter units were sent to the Eastern Front in the spring of 1941 and the fighter forces in the West were forced to go on the defensive again because they were severely reduced in strength. Fighter Wings JG 2 and JG 26 remained in the West to become well known to the Allied Air Forces because of their superior combat record. At the time the *Luftwaffe* was not even aware that these units were the beginning of the Defense of the *Reich* because the air war of the period always took place over the Western Coastal areas and there was very little aerial activity in the skies back toward the homeland.

By the very nature of the offensive role of the fighter forces during 1939 and 1940, there was no need to develop the communications network so necessary for any defensive fighter operations, so this very important aspect was neglected. When the Russian campaign began to falter and the *Luftwaffe* was forced to go on the defensive, demands were made for great increases in all communications facilities but the long lead times necessary to supply them made it impossible to provide much in the short time available. If enough fighter forces had been available in Russia, it would have been possible to live with a reasonable lack of communications, but even though the Western Front was almost drained of fighters, the situation in the air still became a disaster which spread completely throughout Europe. Initially, the *Luftwaffe* had only planned for the shift in forces from West to East to last for just a few weeks, but when the requirement for additional forces stretched on through 1941 and 1942 other areas requiring an increase in fighter forces had to suffer because there were none available.

1942 was the decisive year in the struggle for air superiority in the West. This was the year that Germany lost the struggle even though the German fighter pilot had done more than his share by the end of that year. Many of the *Luftwaffe* leaders came to the conclusion that the air battle was lost when the United States Army Air Forces first appeared and the air offensive against Germany split into strikes conducted in the day by Americans and night missions were conducted by the RAF starting in the second half of the year. The German High Command was totally unable to plan for any counter to meet this kind of aerial offensive, and they were only able to provide momentary stop-gaps for even the most urgent problems. Since the entire focus had to be toward Russia in the East by necessity even though the High Command had correctly estimated the threat from the West, the Germans considered that the defeat of Russia was the only way the entire war could have been continued. As a result, the *Luftwaffe* fell further and further behind in trying to combat a strategic air war until finally, in 1944 when the High Command came to grips with the situation and began to take the necessary steps to counter act.

When the first attacks by four-engine bombers began against occupied countries in the West in late summer of 1942, there were only three fighter Wings with about 120 aircraft each operating on the Channel and in Holland. JG 2 and JG 26 had been fighting in the air since Dunkirk and had been joined by JG 1 while gaining experience in combating both escorted and unescorted enemy heavy bomber formations. There were no fighter units available back in Germany except for two operational training units in the West and South, but neither of these had any operational capabilities. The two OTU's plus flights organized from factory test pilots as well as a few instructor flights from fighter training schools could put up a very limited capability. They were not tied into the normal communications and operational command structure, so they could not be used with any success against escorted Allied heavy bomber formations.

The first attack by the USAAF Bomber Forces took place on the 17th of August, 1942, when 6 B-17Es, escorted by a strong force of RAF Spitfires provided a diversion for a main attack force of 12 Fortresses bound for Rouen, France to bomb a locomotive workshop. Four Squadrons of Spitfires provided close escort cover en route to the target. The German fighter forces did not attempt to make intercept, and no aircraft were lost during this Mission. Although the target was just a short distance away from England to allow for escort by the short ranged Spitfires, the Command structure of the Eighth Air Force was exuberant because there were no losses, and it was felt that this attack portended great things for the future.

However, an the 9th of October, 1942, this vision was partially destroyed when heavy bombers of the Eighth Air Force were targeted to bomb the Five-Lillie Steel Works in Belgium with 108 aircraft in the main strike force and an additional 7 providing a diversion. A heavy force of RAF and USAAF fighters including three Lockheed Lightning P-38

Squadrons of the 1st Fighter Group supported the bomber formations from mid channel back to England, but the *Luftwaffe* only attacked the heavy bombers when they were without escort during penetration and over the target. Four Allied aircraft were lost, but the rest of the crews submitted claims of 56 enemy aircraft destroyed, 26 more probably destroyed and another 20 damaged. This number constituted more aircraft than the total German fighter force participating in the mission. A later revision of these claims on the part of the Allies finally gave credit for 21 aircraft destroyed, 21 others probably destroyed, and 15 damaged, but actually only two German fighters were lost through enemy action and no others were damaged. However, this attack was considered to be only the beginning by the *Luftwaffe*, and the fighter forces were ordered to concentrate on developing the best possible-methods of attacking the heavily armed four-engine American bombers.

By the end of 1942, the Americans had conducted 30 missions over enemy held territory, but none had penetrated Germany proper. In between these sporadic raids by the USAAF heavy bomber forces, the Allies conducted fighter sweeps over the English Channel and the Low Countries. These efforts were generally uneventful because the *Luftwaffe* considered them to be little more than a nuisance and only tried to make contact on an average of one mission out of five. Whenever contact was actually made both sides tried to feel each other out. Because the USAAF brought new and untried aircraft into combat the *Luftwaffe* pilots wanted every opportunity to compare the Bf 109 and the Fw 190 with the P-38s and P-47s flown by the American pilots.

On January 27th, 1943, the USAAF penetrated Germany for the first time by attacking Wilhelmshaven with a force of 64 B-17s. The *Luftwaffe* responded with Bf 109s and Fw 190s while twin-engine fighter aircraft approached the bomber formations but did not attack. One B-17 and two B-24s were lost from this small force, but the *Luftwaffe* came to the correct conclusion that daylight attacks would soon be hitting targets on the North Sea Coast as well as Northeast Germany. To counter these anticipated thrusts against the homeland on April 1st, 1943, JG 1, the fighter force guarding the Northwest German Seaboard, was split to make a new Fighter Wing designated JG 11. These units, based in the Bremen area, were equipped with both the Fw 190 and the Bf 109 and were the first to fly on defensive missions over Germany proper since the RAF had made the daylight attacks during the Polish campaign. At this time more *Luftwaffe* units were being withdrawn from other fronts until the strength of the fighter forces in Northwest Germany, France and the Low Countries rose from 270 aircraft in April, 1943 to 630 aircraft in August, only f our months later. By this time the Eighth Air Force had 570 B-17s in 16 combat groups which were capable of launching 400 aircraft for any one mission.

On May 14th, 1943, the Eighth Air Force changed tactics to provide fighter escort throughout an entire bombing mission when 118 P-47s escorted 60 B-17s to the General Motors Plant at Antwerp, Belgium. Spitfires escorted the bombers across the channel each way to the limit of their range. The fighters were instructed to fly with squadrons in trail, sweeping in behind the bombers, then passing over the top of the formation and then returning directly to home base. Although no heavy bombers were lost, the Allied fighters claimed two Fw 190s destroyed while losing three P-47s to enemy action. In spite of these small claims, this raid had a far reaching effect on the *Luftwaffe* because JG 27 and JG 3 were immediately transferred back into Germany with all their groups in order to provide protection for the Ruhr and the basins of the Rhein and Main Rivers. In addition two high altitude Wings were established to combat high flying reconnaissance aircraft. JG 25 was located in the Berlin area while JG 50 was located in the Rhine-Main Basin. Both were equipped with the Bf 109G-5 that had a pressure cabin and Methanol injection for the engines.

Until late summer the Eighth Air Force had tried to complicate each raid with diversionary attacks and feints in hopes that the *Luftwaffe* would be fooled into heading in the wrong direction away from the main bomber formations. At the same time strategic planners had been considering bombing vital ball bearing production facilities inside Germany and had additionally contemplated attacks on aircraft production facilities at the same time. These deliberations finally led to a mission on August 17, 1943 when bombers of the 4th Wing attacked the Messerschmitt factory at Regensburg while flying on to land at bases in North Africa. At the same time bombers of the 1st Wing undertook a parallel mission of striking the ball bearing factories at Schweinfurt with a return to England. 147 B-17s were dispatched to Regensburg and 230 were directed to Schweinfurt. About 200 *Luftwaffe* fighters made interceptions during these attacks.

Two groups of P-47s provided penetration support to the German border, but another group miscalculated the rendezvous time and left the bombers at the rear unprotected. The *Luftwaffe* was able to begin attacks on the rear of the formation in the area of Brussels continuing all the way to the target and on the withdraw until two more groups of P-47s picked up the returning bombers some 15 miles East of Europe. The *Luftwaffe* used every trick they could muster in attempting to repulse this raid as the fighters made passes on both the noses and tails of the bombers. In addition they dove out of the sun firing at the high squadrons and then continuing on to strike at lower squadrons as well. Unescorted for 150 miles to the target and 150 more during withdrawal, the bomber crews suffered severe punishment as wave after wave of Bf 109s and Fw 190s pressed home attacks, singly, in pairs, and in flights of four or more.

Altogether a total of 60 bombers were lost from the attacking force of 377 aircraft which were dispatched to these two targets. Initially, the USAAF claimed a total of 288 *Luftwaffe* aircraft had been destroyed, but these claims were later reduced to 148. Actually the *Luftwaffe* lost only 27 aircraft during the day. This one mission with a loss rate of almost 16% seemed to vindicate those who advocated that daylight bombing would result in insupportable losses. However, officials on the Allied side felt that a loss rate of 10% could be sustained so they intended to press on with an ever increasing number of bombers in formation. On the other side the leaders of the *Luftwaffe* took immediate action to strengthen their forces in anticipation of a repeat performance.

In his book, *Inside the Third Reich*, Albert Speer, then Minister of Armaments and Production, described the effect the August 17th raid had on the German war industry:

> "Ball bearings had already become a bottle neck in our efforts to increase armaments production. After this attack the production of ball bearings dropped by 38%. Despite the peril to Schweinfurt we had to patch up our facilities there, for to attempt to relocate our ball bearing industry would have held up production entirely for three or four months.
>
> In the light of our desperate needs we could also do nothing about the ball bearing factories in Berlin-Erkner, Cannstatt, or Steyr, although the enemy must have been aware of their location. After

this first blow we were forced back on the ball bearing stocks stored by the armed forces for use as repair parts. We soon consumed these as well as whatever had been accumulated in the factories for current production. After these reserves were used up they lasted for six to eight weeks the sparse production was carried daily from the factories to the assembly plants, often in knapsacks. In those days we anxiously asked ourselves how soon the enemy would realize that he could paralyze the production of thousands of armaments plants merely by destroying five or six relatively small targets."

As a counter measure for this initial attack that included a shuttle raid to North Africa, the *Luftwaffe* sent JG 27 to the Vienna area and JG 3 to the Munich area in September. In addition, *Zerstörer* units with their twin-engine aircraft were also transferred, with ZG 76 going to Southern Germany and ZG 26 going to Northern Germany, both to be used in conjunction with the single-engine fighter units in these areas. Thus, by the time of the second attack on Schweinfurt on the 14th of October, all the fighter and *Zerstörer* forces now stationed in Germany could effectively be brought to bear. The Nazis had been slow to accept the USAAF daylight bombing attacks as a threat to their war industry because Hitler had preferred to believe that the *Luftwaffe* would make these raids too costly to support. However, the many successful bombing missions in the Spring and Summer of 1943 finally convinced the High Command that the situation was urgent. In consequence, the number of single-engine fighters facing the Allies had increased from approximately 300 to nearly 800 by October just before the mission of the 14th.

On that date the USAAF again struck Schweinfurt, but this time with less than 300 B-17s. As before, the P-47's escorting turned back at Aachen and the *Luftwaffe* fighter force struck the formations as soon as the escort departed. Again the attacking force used frontal attacks with the aircraft rolling as they fired at the bombers. In addition, Bf 110s flying astern of the bombers, lobbed rockets at the B-17s. Predicted low clouds gave no relief to the bombers as JG 3 and JG 51 now based near Munich, delivered attack after attack, assisted by large numbers of twin-engine aircraft from the night fighter force based in the Stuttgart and Metz areas. Instead of friendly fighters, Fw 190s met the bombers near the channel coast inflicting heavy damage all because many of the P-47s were grounded by fog. In the end 60 B-17s were missing, 5 had crashed over England, 12 were written off by crash landings, and 121 needed repair. Again these losses were extremely high but the USAAF claimed 288 enemy aircraft destroyed although this figure was later whittled down to 186.

Surprisingly, the leaders of both the *Luftwaffe* and the Allied Air Forces considered this mission to be successful. Albert Speer noted in his book:

> "On October 14th, 1943, I was at the East Prussian Headquarters discussing Armaments questions with Hitler when Adjutant Schaub interrupted us, "The *Reich* Marshal urgently wishes to speak to you, he said to Hitler, "This time he has pleasant news." Hitler came back from the telephone in good spirits. A new daylight raid on Schweinfurt had ended with a great victory for our defenses, he said. The countryside was strewn with downed American bombers. Uneasy, I asked for a short recess in our conference, since I wanted to telephone Schweinfurt myself. But all communications were shattered. I could not reach any of the factories. Finally, by enlisting the police, I managed to talk to the foreman of a ball bearing factory. All the factories had been hard hit, he informed me. The oil baths for the bearings had caused serious fires in the machinery workshops; the damage was far worse than after the first attack. This time we had lost 67% of our ball bearing production."

On the part of the Allies, laying waste to three ball bearing factories together with the destruction of 288 enemy fighters was considered a victory of considerable magnitude. In Britain Air Marshall Portal Chief of the Air Staff, reported: "The Schweinfurt raid may well go down in history as one of the decisive air actions of this war. It may prove to have saved countless lives by depriving the enemy of a great part of his means of resistance." However, under these waves of propaganda there were some hard and unpleasant facts that gave a much different picture.

It was true that 67% of the total ball bearing output of Germany had been destroyed, and it would be six months before the plants could be returned to full production, but the destruction of 186 fighter aircraft was not easy to accept. When this figure was added to the claims made in five major air battles in October the total of over 700 aircraft destroyed and another 300 damaged amounted to the destruction of the total German fighter force. The British Air Ministry Intelligence always had a fair idea of the *Luftwaffe* combat units and they found only an expansion and strengthening of the fighter force during this period. Even though the fighter forces were very hard pressed and had a high rate of attrition, they were demonstrating an increasing ability to break up the close bomber formations and hand out great punishment. The formula of mass concentration of fighters on one bomber formation at a time causing them to break up by firing rockets beyond the range of defensive guns and then pressing home attacks by single-engine fighters had brought excellent results. However, the loss of 20% of the attacking force was twice the rate the Eighth Air Force thought to be prohibitive. This was the last of the four-engine bomber raids that did not have fighter escort in the target area.

About this time Albert Speer was present when a dramatic scene took place between Galland and Göring, and Speer recorded it as follows in his book:

"Adolph Galland had reported to Hitler that several American fighter planes accompanying the bomber Squadrons had been shot down over Aachen. He added the warning that Germany was in grave peril if American fighters, thanks to improved fuel capacity, should soon be able to provide escort protection to the fleets of bombers on flights even deeper into Germany. Hitler had just relayed these points to Hermann Göring. Göring was embarking for Rominten Heath on his special train when Galland came along to bid him good-bye.

"What's the idea of telling the Führer that American fighters have penetrated into the territory of the *Reich*?" Göring snapped at him.

"Herr *Reich*marshal, "Galland replied with imperturbable calm, "They will soon be flying even deeper."

Göring spoke even more vehemently, "That's nonsense, Galland, what gives you such fantasies? That's pure bluff!"

Galland shook his head. "Those are facts, Herr *Reich* Marshal!" As he spoke he deliberately remained in a casual posture, his cap somewhat askew, a long cigar clamped between his teeth. "American fighters have been shot down over Aachen. There is no doubt of it!" Göring obstinately held his ground; "That is simply not true, Galland. It's impossible."

Galland reacted with a touch of mockery: "You might go and check it yourself, Sir; the downed planes are there at Aachen."

Göring tried to smooth matters over. "Come now, Galland, let me tell you something. I'm an experienced fighter pilot myself I know what is possible. But I know what isn't too. Admit you made a mistake." Galland only shook his head, until Göring finally declared:

"What happened is that they were shot down much farther to the West. I mean, if they were very high when they were shot down they could have glided quite a distance farther before they crashed."

Not a muscle moved in Galland's face. "Glided to the East, Sir? If my plane were shot up..."

"Now then, Herr Galland," Göring fulminated, trying to put an end to the debate, "I officially assert that the American fighter planes did not reach Aachen."

The General ventured a last statement: "But, Sir, they were there!"

At this point Göring's self-control gave way. "I herewith give you an official order that they weren't there! Do you understand? The American fighters were not there! Get that! I intend to report that to the *Führer*."

Göring simply let Galland stand there. But as he stalked off he turned once more and called out threateningly: "You have my official order."

With an unforgettable smile, the General replied: "Orders are orders!"

By the beginning of 1944 the Allies continually strengthened their fighter escort, and this made combat against the bomber formations increasingly difficult. This was especially the case with the twin-engine *Zerstörer* fighter units. In the first place these aircraft could not out perform the single-engine fighters of the Allies and in the second place they were sent aloft carrying external fuel tanks and rocket launchers which made them even more vulnerable. By this time most of the German fighter formations were making head on attacks although this type of attack required very good flying and shooting abilities coupled with the ability to fly in very close formation.

For the young and inexperienced fighter pilot who had not received adequate training anyway, these attacks were very dangerous, so the fighter

forces gradually shifted to attacking from the rear as they had done initially when the B-17s first appeared in the skies over Europe. The
Sturmgruppen, which was an organization of pilots with many victories,
pilots who were renegades, pilots who had been given some sort of disciplinary action or volunteers, were very successful in making attacks from
the rear and these tactics became standard for the fighter force. Still, very
close formation flying with a small interval between aircraft, opening fire
from very close range and very good air discipline were the prerequisites
for successful attacks. From the rear on the whole, this type of attack
brought about more victories than the head-on pass because the latter was
so much more difficult.

In January 1944, the *Luftwaffe* had 25 Groups of single engine fighters in the *Reich* and on the Western Front consisting of about 750 aircraft.
In addition there were 7 Groups of twin-engine Destroyers consisting of
about 180 aircraft. The twin-engine fighter force, due to its success with
air to air rockets had been revived, and Bf 110 units had been brought
back from Russia, the Mediterranean, and the Bay of Biscay. Assembling
these aircraft in more confined geographical areas made it possible to use
larger formations called *Gefechtsverband*. The purpose was to bring large
forces of fighters up against the bombers in smaller intervals of time and
space because, until this time, the fighter groups had attacked one after
another instead of all at one time. The *Gefechtsverband*s were located in
four general areas, Holland, Westphalia, and the Rhine, the Rhein-Main
Basin, and the area of Linz, Passau, and Vienna.

In May 1944, the first planned enlargement of Groups in the Defense
of the *Reich* took place. In the Squadrons the number of aircraft were
increased from 12 to 16 and a fourth Squadron was added to each group.
The additional Squadrons were assigned from the Russian front. The
Luftwaffe High Command had been planning for the possibility of putting up 1,000 fighter aircraft on a single mission and the new re-organization would make these missions possible.

These missions which were to be called "Great Blows" had been
very carefully planned and all details had been carefully worked out. Adolf
Galland described the situation thus:

> "All commodores and commanders were called together for a
> rehearsal at the 1st Fighter Corps in Treuenbrietzen, during which

four or five different action and approach flights were practiced with all variations. It was wholly agreed that in the frame of the planned action the following points had to be achieved:

1. In the first action at least 2,000 fighters in 11 combat formations of the 1st Fighter Corps were to be brought into contact with the approaching bomber formations.
2. During the fly-in and the return of the enemy about another 150 fighters of the *Luftwaffe* Command, West were to be sent up.
3. In the second action another 500 fighters were to be brought into contact with the enemy.
4. About 100 night fighters were to screen the borders toward Sweden and Switzerland to catch damaged or straggling single bombers.
5. To shoot down an approximate total of 400 to 500 four-engine bombers against a loss of about 400 aircraft and about 100-150 pilots. These missions were planned to begin in November 1944."

In May 1944, six fighter groups were transferred into the Number Ansback-Wurzburg area to provide an even greater concentration for the *Gefechtsverband* mass missions. The operational control of these units was to come under a special staff of the *Geschwader* that had been set up to control units that were separated from their parent organizations. The centralized position of these groups under the special *Geschwader* made them available to defend against attacks from the South as well as from the West in order to repulse any more shuttle raids between England, Italy, and Africa.

The build up for the 1,000 aircraft missions in Defense of the *Reich* proceeded slowly when the Allies invaded the Continent on June 6,1944. All fighter units with the exception of the new *Geschwader* and the units set up for single-engine night fighting or those converted to day fighting in bad weather were transferred to the West to repulse the invasion. So on the 7th of June there were only 4 regular single-engine fighter units back in Germany to start the Defense of the *Reich*.

On invasion day, a total of 2,362 heavy bomber sorties were flown by Eighth Air Force, but weather and other factors prevented the meager

German fighter force from retaliating and only one B-24 was shot down by anti-aircraft fire on the first raid of the day. On the 7th of June, German fighters were again unable to counter attack as two missions of 500 heavy bombers each conducted tactical mission's in support of the invasion forces. Again just one aircraft was hit by flack and lost during the day. However, the same day at dusk the *Luftwaffe* launched several Me 410 twin-engine aircraft that managed to intermingle with the returning bomber forces to shoot down four B-24s. One Me 410 was shot down by night fighters of the RAF, but this level of effort was all the *Luftwaffe* could dispatch during the first two days of the invasion.

On the 20th of June, 1,402 heavy bombers with an escort of 718 fighters attacked targets in Misburg, Hamburg, Bremen and Hannover as well as additional targets in Politz and Ostermoor. Through all means at their disposal, including radar and the listening watch, the *Luftwaffe* anticipated the attack on Ostermoor and were able to strike with a large force of Bf 110s and Me 410s at a point where Allied Mustangs could not provide escort. As the *Zerstörers* attacked the heavy bombers from the side and rear with rockets, other single-engine fighters were able to evade the escort to attack the retreating bomber formations, and altogether 49 four-engine bombers were shot down while another 400 were damaged. Reorganization of the *Luftwaffe* fighter forces in Defense of the *Reich* was beginning to have an effect.

By the end of June, two additional *Jagdgeschwaders* were combined into a *Gefechtsverband*, and, for the first time since the beginning of the invasion, formations of from 100 to 120 aircraft could be launched simultaneously to give battle in the Defense of the *Reich*. The first successful mission for these formations occurred on July 7,1944.

On this occasion 756 B-17s and 373 B-24s made a return visit to bomb the synthetic oil production facilities at Bohlen, Meiseburg, and Lutzendorf and aircraft factories at Leipzig. Major Wilhelm Moritz's *Sturmgruppe* of JG 3 claimed to have shot down 30 four engine bombers while the *Geschwader* added an additional 24, although only 37 heavies failed to return to England. The *Luftwaffe* was now rapidly gaining the ability to strike the bomber formations at any point where their fighter escort was missing.

From this date on rapid changes were made to compensate for an ever increasing number of sorties directed against the *Wehrmacht* and industrial targets inside Germany. In mid July, a second *Sturmgruppe* was formed and at the end of July a third was created around a cadre from already existing *Sturmgruppe*s. Missions flown during July and August were conducted by these *Sturmgruppe*s only when single-engine escort was provided because the Allies frequently changed tactics making it necessary to provide escort for the attacking *Zerstörer* units. In the meantime back in Germany proper attempts were made to re-build and refresh Groups that had been decimated on the invasion front. Well inside Germany a reserve force of over 700 fighters had been built up for Defense of the *Reich*, but Hitler instead ordered that this reserve be thrown into the invasion front even though Nazi ground forces were already in full retreat.

Despite this, three large *Gefechtsverband* were formed in the North of Germany with units that had been withdrawn from the West. In mid September the Allies carried out their plan to secure a foothold over the Rhine by dropping British forces at Arnheim and two U.S. Divisions from the air at Eindhoven and Nijmegen. When the heavy bombers carrying out tactical bombing to support this operation arrived over their targets the *Luftwaffe* was able to put up big formations of 400 to 500 fighters on the 11th, 12th and 13th of September and they scored a considerable number of victories. Because of the nature of tactical air support by big bombers, the *Luftwaffe* was able to concentrate various *Gefechtsverband* units into the proper time and space against relatively small numbers of Allied bombers. However, these successes were considered to be very expensive because of the large number of German fighters that were shot down by Mustang fighter escort.

In a conference held at Hitler's Headquarters on the 15th of September 1944, the *Geschwader* Commodores demanded a clear division between escort and attack fighters and further insisted upon a ratio of either 3 to 1 or at least 2 to 1 of single-engine to twin-engine fighters. However, Hitler repeated his orders that the principle function of the German fighters was to shoot down bombers and combat with enemy fighter escort was to be avoided. Galland sharply opposed these orders because he felt that it was impossible to attack the bombers in a purely defensive fighter formation. He felt that fighter escort should be provided for the *Sturmgruppe* in a ratio of one single-engine fighter to each twin-engine *Zerstörer*, and he would have had 50 single-engine fighters attacking the enemy fighter escort without trying to give them the additional task of escorting the *Sturmgruppes*. However, Tactical Regulations in line with Hitler's orders were issued as a result of these discussions in spite of Galland's suggestions.

As the German Army was gradually thrown back to the Siegfried Line fighter operations became extremely difficult and very ineffective because of the conditions that existed during the retreat. However, the *Luftwaffe* once again managed to re-group several of the best fighter units with JG 26 at the Northern end of the Siegfried Line, JG 27 in the Bonn area, JG 2 in the Frankfort area, and JG 53 on the Southern end of the Siegfried Line. All of the rest of the *Jagdgeschwader* were located in central Germany around Berlin either conducting missions against attacking Allied bomber formations or attempting to build up strength in spite of all reverses in the air. On the ground, the Fighter Leaders of the *Luftwaffe* believed that a new great effort was entirely possible by realigning all of the fighter *Geschwader* into a concentration of forces around the Berlin area and this might be powerful enough to deal a crippling blow to the Allied Air Armadas. If the Allied Heavy Bomber Force was damaged heavily enough, Germany might have time to produce enough fighter aircraft including jets to turn the tide of the battle in the air against the Allies. In spite of the fact that several large fighter units had to be transferred into the Holland area for combat against the English airborne operations at Arnheim, the High Command feverishly began to prepare for the "Big Blow."

By mid November 1944, the *Geschwader* were up to increased strength. Ten *Jagdgeschwader* under the control of *Jagdkorps* I were organized to attack the Allied bomber forces on the way into the target areas and 3 additional *Jagdgeschwader* under the control of *Jagdkorps* II were to combat the bombers on their way back out of Germany. The forces under both *Jagdkorps* would fly a second mission during each day, so that at least 2,000 fighters of Jagdkorps I would fly on the first mission and 500 on the second mission while *Jagdkorps* II could put up at least 150 fighters. 80 to 100 night fighters were ready to take part by attacking any stragglers. Bad weather intervened to prevent scheduling any "Big Blow" missions throughout the winter months.

Galland recorded what then happened in his book as follows:

"In the middle of November, I received an alarming order, the whole impact of which I could not foresee. The fighter-reserves were to be prepared for action on the front where a great land battle was expected in the West. This was incredible! The whole training had been aimed at action in the Defense of the *Reich*. All new pilots should have had some training in the totally different conditions at the front, but petrol shortage forbade this. With regard to the supply situation it would have been irresponsible to use the stores accumulated for the Big Blow for training purposes. Moreover, the internal organization of the units, the tactics, the armament, and the equipment were only suited for the special task of the Defense of the *Reich*. A readjustment within a fortnight, as had been ordered, could not be undertaken. The experience and standard of the unit leaders and pilots could be regarded as just passable for the Defense of the *Reich*, but for action at the front they were absolutely out of the question. Besides the Squadrons had now without exception a strength of 70 aircraft and were therefore much too large for the airfields at the front.

"On November 20th the transfer to the West was ordered regardless of my scruples and objections only the 300th and 301st Fighter Wings would remain in the *Reich*. I must admit that even now, as I took part in the discussion for the mobilization of the fighters in the West, it had not occurred to me that all these preparations were for our own counter offensive. Until the very last I was kept in the dark and only a few days before the start of the offensive in the Ardennes was I informed of the plan. Only then did I realize that the High Command from the beginning had understood something quite different by the Big Blow, and that the intention to go over to the offensive in the West already existed at the end of July.

"On October 11th, Hitler had been presented with the operational plan that had been worked out by the General Staff and for the most part he sanctioned it. Right from the outset he had guaranteed a strong fighter support for the Army under suppositions that, of course, did not exist. By this time the preparations were much too advanced to make any serious attempt at changes. Also my influence with the High Command had sunk so low that any such attempt would have been hopeless. At the time I was merely tolerated, because no one knew who was to be my successor. The third and last formation of a

reserve was to be the last major task of the General of the Fighter
Arm. The reserve was there; then it was taken away from me."

In late November and early December all of these units had to be
again transferred to the West in support of the Ardennes offensive and
they were consumed in the type of combat for which they had not trained,
had experienced or been equipped. This last ditch effort which eventually
failed completely brought to an end the Defense of the *Reich* even though
the *Luftwaffe* made sporadic efforts to turn back the Allied Air Armadas
right up to the end of the war by using the jet propelled Me 262s.

In retrospect Adolph Galland believed that there were a great number of factors that brought about failure of the Defense of the *Reich*. Most
were due to constant interference by both Hitler and Hermann Göring,
but still others were caused by inadequate decisions on the part of all the
various Headquarters. The major breakdown came about because the
Defense of the *Reich* was only organized at the Headquarters level into
Command and Control organizations and no special fighter units were
assigned to them to fight against attacking bomber formations. In addition almost every kind of decision was made too late to effect the situation and even the decisions that were made did not look to the future.
Although the Command organizations were usually up to strength, the
fighter units were not, and thus they could not match the strength of the
attacking Allied forces.

Naturally, fighting on three fronts prevented any possibility of building up adequate fighter forces on any one front. Since Hitler and Göring
either ignored or failed to recognize the strategic potential of a strong
fighter force, the necessary materials, production, and personnel were
never made available even inside Germany. When the High Command
finally recognized that something had to be done in the summer of 1944,
it was too late. Even when this recognition led to preparations for the first
one thousand fighter aircraft missions these attempts were defeated by
indecision by the High Command or by the over-all combat situation
caused by the advancing Allies.

Without a doubt the most decisive ingredient in the Defense of the
Reich was the American fighter aircraft with its long range. Had they not
been able to penetrate deeply into Germany, the *Luftwaffe* would have
been able to stop the daylight attacks in spite of all the errors made by

Hitler and the High Command. Operational air superiority held by the long ranged American fighters could have been wrested from the Allies by a German fighter arm which was superior in strength, fighting ability, and technical quality, but the means to create such a force was never made available.

The German High Command never did appreciate the role of escort fighter aircraft because they did not do direct damage to Germany. Also they did not appreciate that the German fighter arm could only shoot down Allied bombers when the Allied fighter escort was either weakened by combat or missing altogether. Employing fighters on tactical missions in support of the field forces instead of in Defense of the *Reich* defied the purpose for which the organizational changes to create such a great command structure were made in the first place.

Pilot training and aircraft production never well coordinated, were constantly out of harmony because of the Russian campaign, lack of fuel, and Hitler's interference, but production was wasted on marginal bombers, the V-1 and V-2 missiles, and unsuccessful fighter projects. In addition the *Luftwaffe* never did successfully solve the problems of assembly and control of large fighter formations in all kinds of bad weather because there was never time to devote attention to the proper operational training nor to improve radio navigation aids or communications equipment. The High Command never did appreciate what the fighter force had done to weaken Allied air superiority in spite of all odds, and above all, Hitler did not want to face the consequences to Germany if Allied air superiority was not reversed in favor of the *Luftwaffe*.

In the final analysis all of the armament programs neglected quality for quantity and not enough attention was ever devoted to the development of new fighters with more powerful engines and better performances. Only the Me 262 had the necessary superiority and its development and use in limited numbers could not possibly forestall the final collapse of the *Luftwaffe*. In the final analysis it became obvious that a numerically inferior force can only hold its own by superior quality.

Albert Speer added what seems to be the crowning comment regarding the failure of the top echelon to deal in realities:

"When, on March 22, 1945, Hitler invited me to one of his armaments conferences, I again had Karl Sauer represent me. From his notes, it was clear that he and Hitler had frivolously ignored the realities. Although armaments production had long since come to an end, they occupied themselves with projects as though the whole of 1945 was still at their disposal. For example, they discussed the totally nonexistent crude-steel production and also decided that the 88mm antitank gun for the troops was to be produced in "maximum quantities" and the production of the 21cm mortars was to be increased.

"They gloried over the development of entirely new weapons: a new special rifle for the parachute troops with "maximum ejection speed" of course or a new super caliber 30.5cm mortar. The minutes also recorded an order of Hitler's that five new variants of existing types of tanks were to be demonstrated to him within a few weeks. In addition, he wanted to investigate the effect of Greek fire, known since classical antiquity and he wished to have our jet fighter bomber, the Me 262 rearmed as quickly as possible as a fighter plane. In ordering this last action, he was tacitly conceding the error he had made a year and a half before, when he had persistently refused the advice of all the experts."

CHAPTER TWELVE

Valhalla

When the victorious Allies gave consideration to creation of a new *Luftwaffe* several years after the Great War ended, it was necessary to review the mistakes of the past. To the leaders of the free world it had become apparent that a strong force would be needed if the Russians ever decided to move against the Western World, and a defensively powerful Germany would be an important element in maintaining a balance of power in Europe. Since most world leaders would have reacted strongly against the creation of any offensive capability for Germany, it was obvious that a new *Luftwaffe* capable of and equipped for air defense would be the only acceptable solution. Adequate air defense is centered around fighter aircraft, and, thus, the new *Luftwaffe* should be predominantly fighter equipped. However, it would be necessary to review the background of Germany's defeat in the air once again. Almost any nation could benefit from the lessons learned in the sky over Germany, and those lessons could make a great contribution to any military doctrine suitable for future wars in the air.

The fact that Germany was a dictatorship and the *Luftwaffe* was controlled by a sycophant who refused to deal in realities and would tolerate no adverse information to reach his leader created the backbone of defeat. Because ruthless use of power was so frequently used in the Nazi regime, rational thought had to be shaped to conform to the irrational views of those in power. Logic, planning, management, and performance all suffered interference from above and the individual could too easily become lost in a dream world of unreality passed down from on high.

The greatest mistakes the *Luftwaffe* made were in organizing and planning for the Fighter Force. The German High Command, always fearful of Hitler and Göring did not believe that fighter aircraft would have a significant role in strategic air warfare, and so the fighter forces were always too small in relation to other elements of the *Luftwaffe*. In autumn, 1939, there were 30 bomber groups, 9 dive-bomber groups, and only 13 fighter groups. Because of this grave organizational imbalance, the fighter arm was never considered to be a part of the strategic air force, and, thus, started off in a second rate position. This status was reflected in the lack of proper organization, adequate personnel and materiel, and eventually in combat capability. These unsatisfactory elements all became worse and worse as the war progressed.

Because they had second class status, the fighter forces were never allowed to assign capable individuals to positions of responsibility in the High Command. The officers who became Inspectors of the Fighter Forces, the equivalent of Commanders, were not of top caliber. Even if they had been, they were re-assigned so often that it was virtually impossible to maintain the continuity that could have made the office important. This was especially damaging just when the *Luftwaffe* was preparing for war because, at that time, it was vitally necessary to make decisive and important judgments. During the build up, attack and finally defense, the German fighters were never consolidated into an over all Fighter Command and this became a tremendous organizational disadvantage.

Before the start of the war, the *Luftwaffe* tried to organize and train the fighter force too rapidly by lowering the standards for formation leaders and pilots in the training programs. When war actually began, there were only nine fighter Wings and there were no plans to create additional units until 1942. However, from 1942 to 1944, eight new Wings were organized and the total force was increased even further by increasing the strength of existing units. These increases were made in spite of the rising losses of men and materiel but were found to be necessary to keep even numerically with the enemy. Naturally, the battle potential and combat performance really suffered. The build up was organizationally well conceived, but it came too late considering that nothing had been done to enlarge the fighter force during the two previous victorious years of 1940 and 1941.

In 1941 there were only two small fighter pilot training schools, so it was virtually impossible to train large numbers of good pilots. The High Command only reacted to combat developments instead of planning ahead, and this was especially evident during the build up for the Defense of the *Reich* when almost every one began to panic. Command indecision's resulted in at least a one and one half year delay in this build up and had a domino effect which delayed the development of radar equipment and other technical devices which were urgently required to combat the great enemy forces in the air.

The High Command never did grasp the concept of "Control of the Air" because they only thought in terms of a set piece grand strategy of aerial warfare that allowed for no improvisation or change. The *Luftwaffe* command level never did realize or admit that it was absolutely necessary to establish air superiority for all branches of the Armed Forces especially the air force to be victorious. If this philosophy had been accepted in the early stages of the war, the GAF would have been directed to re-gain air superiority over the Allies when it was first taken away at El Alamein. Instead of taking direct and appropriate action in a concrete way, the High Command began to insult the morale and bravery of the members of the fighter arm. Obviously, this could only be counter-productive.

Since there was never an operational suitability section anywhere in the *Luftwaffe* which was really able to test experimental developments, all sorts of mistakes were constantly made in the design and production of aircraft and associated technical equipment. In 1940 any new development including aircraft which could not be introduced into the units within two years were set aside in order to accelerate those things which had more immediate promise. This was a tremendous mistake which had far reaching effect on the development of the Me 262, further development of the Fw 190, development of engines of more than 2,000 horsepower, the gyro computing gun sight and many other equally important new projects.

Since the High Command insisted on only increasing production of existing types, it was difficult to inject new improvements into the assembly lines at the expense of a production slow down. In addition, each time there was an interesting technical innovation, the High Command became smug and self satisfied, a feeling which would then permeate throughout the entire staff. For this reason the Bf 109 which lacked performance was not taken out of production for years after it became absolutely necessary in early 1943. Similarly, there was a delay in starting a new series of Fw 190 and production of the Ta 152. By the time these decisions were made, they were not effective on the outcome of the war.

The High Command did recognize finally that there were not enough fighter aircraft toward the end of 1943, and then, thanks to the efforts of Albert Speer. A great increase in series production was hastily initiated, but until that time the published monthly production figures were considered to be a joke by all the members of the Fighter Forces. It was a real tribute to the German war effort that the greatest production was actually reached after the aircraft factories and synthetic oil plants had been heavily damaged. However, by that time, the aircraft losses were so huge that any increase in production came too late to forestall defeat. The situation was really complicated by the loss of air superiority which in turn meant heavy losses to ground attack, reconnaissance, and night fighter units because they all required a constant flow of replacement aircraft in order to be effective, and this took away from supplying the fighter arm. The High Command insisted on producing bombers and other associated multi-engine aircraft in order to placate Hitler, so a clear commitment to the production of fighters was delayed until mid 1944. The series production of the wooden He 162 was a clear sign of the decay in logical thinking and planning because the entire industrial capacity should have been devoted to producing the Me 262 that was a vastly superior aircraft.

Throughout the entire war, the *Luftwaffe* High Command consistently repeated technical mistakes and committed the Air Force to ineffective programs because of over-confidence, ignorance, or radical input from Hitler. By 1940, it was obvious that the fighter forces required external fuel tanks to operate over England. Engines capable of maximum performance at least three thousand feet higher than those being flown in the Battle of Britain were a must. Production should have been accelerated at that time for the Fw 190 because these aircraft were urgently needed for escort missions. Any method of temporarily boosting engine performance should have been developed as rapidly as possible. The GAF should also have developed the capability to transmit and receive radio communications between bomber and fighter aircraft because it would have increased fighter control procedures immeasurably. None of these things were done until quite some time after the Battle of Britain had ended. When it was obvious that converting the Bf 109 units to the Fw 190 was an extreme necessity, the change over proceeded quite slowly because the *Wermacht* anticipated victory on all fronts during the 1941 to 1942 time period.

By 1943, it was obvious that fighters would need heavier armament to stop the ever increasing attacks by Allied heavy bombers forces. It was even more obvious that it was necessary to increase the range and power of fighter aircraft by any means available. Accuracy had to be increased by developing gyro computing gun sights so that pilots would be able to shoot down more aircraft considering that they were less and less adequately trained. There never were enough aircraft of any kind so when series production of newer and higher performance fighters actually started, the High Command did not want to take any older aircraft out of production. As a result, great numbers of pilots lost their lives flying obsolescent machinery.

By 1944, production of the earlier versions of the Fw 190 should have stopped entirely to be replaced by the Fw 190D. Series production should also have been started on the Ta 152 as well as the fighter version of the Me 262. It should have been apparent to all that it would be necessary to increase the fuel production for the Me 163 because this little aircraft had excellent combat capabilities, but this was never done. The *Luftwaffe* Fighter Force had always required automatic pilots so they could operate in bad weather since the Allies were able to bomb accurately through the clouds, but, here again, nothing was done to produce such equipment despite the overwhelming number of crashes that occurred due to bad weather. During this same period, it was absolutely necessary to start production of the Dornier 335 because it was an excellent twin-engine destroyer, but even this obvious decision was delayed until it was too late.

The *Luftwaffe* made continuous mistakes in selecting and training personnel for fighter training schools. The High Command did not recognize the necessity to establish very high standards for fighter pilots because Hitler and Göring always insisted that the bomber arm should be given the highest priority in the allotment of the best personnel. When it came to the selection of fighter pilot trainees, the physical and mental standards were set much too low and as a result the small numbers of officers who were actually sent to the fighter forces were inadequately trained. It was quite difficult to select superior formation leaders from the officer corps for this very reason.

Since the training facilities increased six fold during the war, there never was enough fuel set aside for flying training even though there were enough aircraft available for this purpose up until 1944. As a result, the pilots who did graduate from flying training did not have enough flying hours and thus were inadequately trained. As the war progressed, no emphasis was placed on stringent specialized training for the fighter pilot even though these were the very people on whose shoulders rested the potential to turn back the ever increasing numbers of attacking Allied aircraft. The total training program should have been directed toward producing only fighter pilots, but the High Command never realized that this was absolutely necessary to stave off defeat in the air. Increased losses of fighter pilots, especially after 1943, should have been a dire warning to the High Command, and the training programs should have been vastly improved accordingly because young pilots no longer had the opportunity to augment their training by actual experience in the operational units. It all finally became a problem that could never be solved. The low standards of training were obvious to all but the High Command because there was such a low level of experience in the operational units. They consistently flew poor formations in operational aircraft, completely lacked any gunnery and combat skills, and above all, had a total lack of any instrument flying capability.

Since the training programs were not able to produce a reserve of formation leaders, it became necessary to bring these leaders up through the ranks. After 1943, this alternative became impossible because the over all quality of officers in the units was so poor that the wings were not able to locate any leaders who were even remotely qualified. The *Luftwaffe* finally did try to establish a systematic, regularly scheduled training program for formation leaders which should have been done at the beginning not the end of the war, and this effort turned out to be a sort of "University of Fighter Operations."

Even before the war there were very few officers who were adequately trained as Group and Wing Commanders, so pilots whose experience went back to World War I were used instead. These people could not be expected to lead their men in the air because of their age and lack of modern combat experience, so it became necessary to replace many of them during the Battle of Britain. In this rejuvenation process there was no normal evolution of formation leaders. It would have been much better in the long run to have started the process during peacetime, or at least to have proceeded at a slower pace, but the requirement became urgent because of the events in the skies over England.

During the first year of the war there was no Headquarters structure representing Fighter Command, but, during the French Campaign, Fighter Commanders were integrated into a Flying Corps which had very little influence on combat operations. However, they gained power and influence during the Battle of Britain, and, when it became necessary to defend the Continent, the *Jafu*'s and Fighter Division Staff did actually control operations. Combat effectiveness always suffered when this happened because there were very few accomplished, battle experienced commanders who could be assigned to these tasks. All staff officers should have had operational experience in the war, and they should have been trained as pilots or staff officers before moving up to these assignments. Training of general staff officers for the Fighter Force was neglected right up to the very last stages of the war. Worse still, as the war progressed, Göring relieved many, many *Jafu*'s and Fighter Division Commanders from their positions for all sorts of personal reasons. As long as he was Commander in Chief answering only to Hitler, it was impossible for the commanders below him to gain the necessary experience and yet have the peace of mind to do a proper job.

Even though the Fighter Force fought against a numerically superior force on every front, very little effort was ever made to win back air superiority. Instead the fighter forces were required to escort bombers, fighter-bombers, and ground attack units, as they, in turn supported the Army Ground Forces. Time and time again the High Command transferred fighter groups here and there based on the main ground battle effort instead of regarding the Fighter Wings as strike-forces within themselves. As a result, the Groups always went into combat in a confused manner. The influence of a competent wing organizational structure was always missing and the fighters lost much of their operational value. When the fighter forces were sent off to the Russian Front in 1941 at the start of the offensive, the remaining units were able to continue successful operations on the Western Front for a period of time. Eventually, air superiority passed over to the English, and, finally, more decisively to the Americans. At the beginning of the defense of the *Reich*, there appeared to be great possibilities, but these efforts were doomed to failure because there were never enough fighters to turn back the attack of the Allied four-engine bombers. The High Command would never order the withdrawal of all fighter forces from the South and the East in order to defend the homeland, but, instead, transferred Groups back to Germany piecemeal, one by one. As a result the fighter units were always behind the mounting fury of the aerial action and were never able to catch up.

The High Command neglected to build up ground organizations with the necessary communications networks in the rear areas in anticipation of shrinking boundaries caused by defeat after defeat. In retreats and during the build up for the Defense of the *Reich*, all units continually encountered shortages of everything. When operations were curtailed in bad weather, the fighter units were completely over taxed because they lacked experience, were improperly trained, and did not have the proper equipment to fly under these conditions. Resultant heavy losses shook the confidence of the High Command and caused great morale problems throughout the fighter forces. In defending the *Reich*, the High Command demanded that every large attack be met by all available forces regardless of the weather, the weakness of each unit, or the disruption of the entire fighter organization and no attention was given to the independent routes taken by the attacking formations. Thus they never did allow for an economic employment of strength which, in turn, would have provided commanders the opportunity to re-build combat weary and ineffective units. As a result, groups that were especially hard hit by the enemy, lost all effectiveness and were unable to fight as cohesive organizations for all time.

The High Command insisted on employing twin-engine fighters in spite of the fact that they fell easy prey to rapidly increasing numbers of American Fighters. Both Hitler and Göring insisted on using the 5cm cannon on this type of aircraft and this only added to the already very heavy losses. In 1944 the *Luftwaffe* tried three times to form a large reserve of aircraft and pilots so that gigantic mass attacks could be launched against the attacking Allied bomber formations. This would be much like reserve divisions are thrust into land battles to blunt enemy attacks. All three times the opportunity to use these reserves was taken away by a change in orders coming down from Hitler through Göring before there could possibly be a chance for demonstrated success. The first reserve force had to be thrown into the battle when the invasion took place and it was decimated against such great odds. The second reserve was thrown into France in August 1944, and it had no effect at all against the Allied Forces. The third, and by far the largest, reserve which had been trained and equipped for the "Big Blow" operation for Defense of the *Reich*, was thrown into the Ardennes Offensive and torn to pieces.

Of course, there was no other choice but to try and forestall the invasion, but in the other two cases, wasting these forces was a fatal mistake. These fighters could have been much more effectively employed in defending the German homeland instead. Any development of large reserves required long lead times, but the High Command never had the courage to "bite the bullet" by temporarily restricting the activities of the fighter forces until they could be re-built in order to direct effective strikes against the enemy. Just at the time the future was hanging in the balance, the bomber units of the *Fliegerkorps* were absorbed en masse into the existing fighter structure and this became the final fatal blow to the *Luftwaffe* fighter forces. When General Peltz, the leader of the bomber attacks against England and a man whose entire experience was in the bomber forces, was given command of the Second *Jagdkorps* just before the Ardennes Offensive, it was obvious that the entire fighter force faced dissolution and ruin.

During the last several years of the war, both Hitler and Göring desperately searched for scapegoats within the ranks of the *Luftwaffe*, so they both could shift the blame for continued failures in the sky over Germany away from themselves. As the air continually filled with enemy aircraft the German propaganda machine heaped abuse on the fighter pilot, who, it was claimed, lacked courage in the face of enemy fire. Prom the moment air superiority was lost on all fronts, Göring, as the Commander in Chief of the *Luftwaffe*, permitted no realistic reflection, argument or decision to prevail. He always stood in between Hitler and realism and would only provide his leader with news that reflected credit upon himself. Göring continually insisted on insulting the fighter Force to disguise his own failures, and, as a result every individual in Germany believed that it was the fighter force that had failed. It was possible that

Göring thought that insults would taunt the fighter pilot into heroic achievements that would ultimately win the support of the people, but his outspoken criticism had just the opposite effect. In the end the fighter pilot fell into disgrace.

Where ever gasoline supplies and runways permitted take offs, the German fighter pilots kept flying against the Allies until the morning of VE day. They fought a long, hard war with courage, chivalry, and fairness. They were decent men and fair men, but it had been their misfortune to be lumped historically with the perpetrators of German non-military violence. They observed the bonds that must continue to exist between man and man, both in the air and on the ground. Their soldierly conduct in wartime still stands untarnished. They lost the war, but they did not lose their souls, and in the after math they helped build a better Germany. But the path was very long and very hard, and along the way most suffered and many died for reasons that had nothing at all to do with war in the air.

When the war ended, many Fighter Commanders surrendered their entire organizations to the British and Americans in hopes that they would escape being captured by the Russians. However, the Potsdam Accords had divided Germany and a large number of these same units were turned over to the Russians even though they had surrendered to the Western Allies initially. As a divided Germany began to emerge from the ruins to function again, many surviving fighter pilots found themselves living in the Eastern Zone under the communist yoke where it was virtually impossible to find any sort of employment. The USSR considered the German fighter pilots had been responsible for the extremely heavy losses of Russian aircrews during the war and thus were war criminals.

In the West, the fighter pilot returning to his home, found that he was faced with discrimination because of the criticism heaped on his branch of the service during the war. It was almost impossible to find employment because of the stigma attached to all fighter pilots although many had never been employed at anything else during an entire lifetime. It became necessary for each to accept any sort of menial task just to survive. While the plight of the ex-fighter pilot was very difficult, the widows and orphans of fallen fighter pilots were subjected to worse conditions. Former high ranking commanders waited on tables, worked as servants, became janitors, or helped in the reconstruction of destroyed cities. Times were difficult for all Germany let alone a returned service man that had once been a fighter pilot.

Under the guidance of the NATO Nations, reconstruction of West Germany came about at a far more rapid pace than it did in the East under the tutelage of Russia. Relations between the NATO countries and Russia were always strained, and eventually the Russians and the East German Government blockaded Berlin. When the Berlin airlift had shown the Russians that they could not force the British, French and Americans from that city, nor could they force the German residents to give in to communism, the entire German nation felt a new sense of purpose and a responsibility to the European Community of Nations.

Because of the growing pressure and increased military strength, of the Russians in East Germany, it became apparent to the NATO nations that efforts should be directed to give Germany autonomy in government, and to allow the nation to build up a defensive military force. It fell upon representatives of the United States Air Forces occupying Germany to attempt to locate ex-members of the *Luftwaffe* with a view of using them to re-construct a German Air Force. Because Germany is relatively small geographically, any new German military organization would be restricted to defense, so emphasis was placed on developing a primarily fighter equipped air force. Eventually, a nucleus of former German fighter pilots expressed an interest in creating a new *Luftwaffe* in response to the will of the German people.

In the meantime, Adolf Galland and other ex-members of the German Fighter Force had decided to form an association dedicated to assisting all known ex-fighter pilots to find satisfactory jobs. Other objectives were to provide support for the widows and orphans and to assist pilots now living behind the Iron Curtain to escape into West Germany. An additional objective was to restore the reputation of the fighter pilot in the eyes of the whole German population.

As the German Fighter Pilot's Association began to grow, the members made every effort to locate all that had been captured by the Russians and extensive plans were made for entire families to escape as soon as they had been located and identified. Since a few members of the Association came from wealthy families who had established and flourishing businesses, they had not suffered financially because of the war, so they were instrumental in locating adequate jobs for others who were either under employed or not employed at all. Efforts were directed toward helping each new member find suitable housing near his place of employment. When an ex-fighter pilot was located in East Germany he was assisted to escape only after he was assured of a job and suitable accommodations had been arranged for him and his family. The Association became directly involved in fund raising and large amounts of money were given to widows and orphans of fighter pilots who had been killed in action. No needy family was denied.

Eventually, the Association began to publish, a monthly magazine, "The *Jägerblatt*" which featured editorials on the current political scene within Germany, news of members, status of attempts to form a new *Luftwaffe*, and any other up to date information which would be of interest to members. Eventually, all known ex fighter pilots that had been trapped behind the Iron Curtain were spirited out of East Germany and provided with living and working conditions in the West. The climax of this endeavor came when Erich Hartmann, the top ranking *Luftwaffe* Fighter Ace, credited with the destruction of 352 enemy aircraft, was released after 10 years of prison inside Russia.

When the *Luftwaffe* eventually became functional, many members of the German Fighter Pilot's Association became unit commanders. Many top-ranking aces of the old *Luftwaffe* became senior staff officers who were instrumental in building the new fighter forces into an efficient air defense combat team. Adolf Galland, though effective in behind the scene activities, made little effort to rejoin, but began to enter into the political arena to insure that there would be a general acceptance of the new *Luftwaffe* by the entire German population. Eventually, the heroic role of the fighter pilot emerged.

The German Fighter Pilot's Association currently consists of retired and active duty members including several fighter pilots who survived World War II. Over 800 pilots who shot down more than 5 enemy aircraft have been identified and located. In 1961 the Association erected a memorial in the shape of an obelisk topped by two bronze eagles dedicated to "Fallen Fighter Pilots of the World." The Association holds annual conventions in convenient locations in Germany where members relive old memories and devise ways to help better the new *Luftwaffe*. Many members have achieved social and political prominence and others are wealthy even by German standards. Each succeeding Chief of Staff of the new *Luftwaffe* had been a member of the Fighter Pilot's Association and many have outstanding combat records including experiences during World War II.

In 1961 the new *Luftwaffe* was predominantly fighter aircraft equipped, and represented the evolution learned from the lessons of World War II. By 1961 there were 111,000 men in the German Air Force structure, and the fighter force consisted of 26 Squadrons. There were four Squadrons of F-84Fs (60 aircraft) for ground attack, eight Squadrons of F-104G1s (144 aircraft) for escort of air superiority, five Squadrons of Fiat G-91's (102 aircraft) used for ground support, four Squadrons of All Weather F-84Fs (60 aircraft), one Interceptor Squadron of F-104G1s (18 aircraft), four reconnaissance Squadron of RF-4Fs (60 aircraft) for a total of 444 fighter aircraft. In addition the *Luftwaffe* had five transport Squadrons of 76 aircraft, 4 helicopter Squadrons with 105 UH-1D's, 8 Pershing Surface to Air Missile Squadrons, 24 Nike-Hercules surface to air batteries, and 4 Air Control and Warning Regiments.

The 444 aircraft of the new *Luftwaffe* appeared to be quite small compared to the strength of the old *Luftwaffe* at the beginning of World War II. Then, there were 1,180 Bombers, 771 Single Seat Fighters, 336 Dive-bombers, 408 Twin-Engine Escort Destroyers, and 379 Reconnaissance aircraft for a total force of 3,074 aircraft. But between 1939 and 1945, the *Luftwaffe* lost 94,500 aircraft of all types including 38, 900 fighters, 9,800 night fighters, and 21,800 bombers. During this period, 138, 596 officers and men of the *Luftwaffe* were killed in action, and 156,132 were listed as missing and presumed dead. They had trusted Adolf Hitler and were rewarded by him with an early death. It is now believed that only 4,000 to 5,000 men who belonged to the *Luftwaffe* during World War II survived.

The German Fighter Pilot's Association made tremendous efforts to identify and verify the combat records of top ranking German fighter pilots during the war years, and this search led to the publication of a book covering the exploits of 586 fighter pilots who were awarded various versions of the Knight's Cross, which was a higher class of the Iron Cross, the coveted "Blue Max." In addition, extensive research was directed toward determining the loss and victory rates of the Allies as compared to the German Fighter Arm. The comparison that emerged is almost unbelievable and has met with considerable skepticism. Since the

Germans always encountered almost overwhelming air superiority on all fronts, the historical facts are astonishing.

In the year's 1941 and 1942, two *Luftwaffe* Fighter Wings, JG 2 and JG 26 equipped with only some 80 to 120 fighter aircraft had the responsibility for defense along the entire Western Front between the Netherlands and the Bay of Biscay. In North Africa the entire German aerial campaign was conducted by just one fighter wing. In Russia there were never more than 400 to 600 operational day fighters from 1941 to 1944. On June 6th 1944, the day of the invasion, there were only 90 German fighters in the West to offer opposition to 5,400 fighters of the USAAF and the RAF. Within a few weeks after the invasion, this limited German force was increased to 600 aircraft, but these were almost all eliminated in a very short time. In spite of the Allied numerical superiority, the German fighters were able to achieve a balance until the end of 1943, but this was only because of superior flying ability and superb fighting spirit of the fighter pilots. By the end of 1943, under-trained fighter pilots had no chance to survive against a numerically and technically superior enemy.

From 1939 to 1945, German fighter pilots reported shooting down approximately 25,000 British, French and American aircraft in addition to 45,000 which were piloted by Russians. Although there are no accurate loss figures for the Russian Air Force, both the RAF and the USAAF officially reported over 40,000 losses for this period. The Allies sent more than 20,000 aircraft to Russia and the Russians themselves were able to produce approximately 2,000 aircraft per month from the first of 1942 until the end of the war. Thus in three years they had produced over 76,000 aircraft. The Russians probably had 140,000 aircraft in operation during the entire war, so the 77,000 aircraft reported destroyed by the German authorities are probably correct. The Germans have estimated that 120,000 Russian aircraft were brought down with anti aircraft batteries accounting for 20,000 of this total. The remainder was credited to German day and night fighter pilots.

One hundred and five German fighter pilots were credited with over one hundred victories each in combat and they had a combined total of 15,000 aircraft destroyed between them. An additional 360 day and night fighter pilots reported between forty and one hundred victories each for a combined total of 21,000 enemy aircraft destroyed. Another five hundred pilots were credited with 20 to 40 victories each thus adding another 15,000 downed aircraft to the total and over 2,500 fighter pilots could have been called aces because they had downed five or more enemy aircraft. In the last six months of the war, the entire German reporting system collapsed, so it was virtually impossible to make any sort of tabulation of aerial victories which could have been added to the known totals during that period.

It is well to remember that the destruction of each enemy aircraft in combat had to be confirmed by the Commander in Chief of the German Air Force. Each victory was initially confirmed by either aerial or ground witnesses unless the crashed aircraft itself was located or the members of its crew were taken prisoner. The combat report had to be endorsed by the immediate superior officer after which it was sent to the Wing Staff and from there to the *Luftwaffe* Ministry. The bureaucratic system could take up to one year or even longer to confirm. The system did, however, keep human mistakes and weaknesses within limits. Aerial dogfights were usually swift, turbulent and confusing, and it was often impossible to keep an aircraft that had been seemingly been destroyed in sight until it crashed. Not all German aircraft had gun cameras capable of photographing the aerial action because this equipment was given to only a very few privileged experts. Ambition and a desire to be famous could lead to erroneous claims, but these were more or less evened out by a great number of victories that could never be claimed because there had been no witnesses.

The Germans established a commission to receive all reports of aircraft wreckage found by search units. Since fighter pilots and anti-aircraft units often claimed more victories than were actually accounted for, this commission checked on all claims and awarded a kill to only one party or individual. Certainly, no more confirmations were awarded than wrecks accounted for, and it is wrong to conclude that eventual confirmations were exaggerated. Exorbitant daily figures issued by the War Ministry during the war years were often caused by double reporting or the desire to report victoriously to the German people.

Over the years so much attention has been directed to the few German fighter pilots who were given great recognition because they had one, two or even three hundred enemy aircraft destroyed that it is easy to overlook what actually happened to the German Fighter Arm. Their losses were within acceptable limits during the years of 1939 to 1942, but they became unbearable in 1943 and finally led to complete attrition. Altogether 22, 500 day-fighter aircraft were lost to enemy action with another non-combat operational losses occurring during the years 1939 to 1945.

In addition, 4,800 destroyer and night fighter aircraft were lost to the enemy and an additional 6,200 were lost in operational accidents. Altogether 10,800 pilots were known to have been killed in combat. JG 26 lost a total of 805 pilots and JG 27 lost 823 which meant that they lost over six times their total assigned number during their operational history. After 1943 the chances for survival of fighter pilots were slim indeed, and one fourth of them did not survive their first four missions.

In the final analysis 569 fighter pilots shot down a total of over 35,500 enemy aircraft in combat and these included 1800 four-engine bombers. These 568 men were all holders of the Knight's Cross and 296 of them were either killed in action from 1939 to 1945, were reported missing, or had fatal accidents. Nineteen holders of the Knight's Cross who had been held in captivity before 1945 returned to Germany after the war. Most of the survivors suffered greatly from serious combat injuries. Far from being Hitler's fall guys, over 2,500 German fighter pilots, whether they held the Knight's Cross or not, certainly were qualified as heroes and should have been thus recognized by the people of Germany.

Adolf Galland perhaps paid the best tribute to the German fighter pilots who were killed in combat when he outlined his beliefs of the requirements for good fighter pilots the world over:

"The fighter pilot must always take the offensive and be aggressive and when this requirement is over looked as is the case when fighters are required to provide purely defensive escort for other types of aircraft, a great tactical error will be committed. Even in defense the fighter pilot must not avoid combat but must accept it, other wise he turns the advantage to the enemy. There should never be a fixed tactical plan for fighter operations; surprise, cunning, and maneuverability must always be combined with aggressiveness and dash. These ingredients must be exhibited by Commanders at all times and under all circumstances.

In the final analysis when history has examined the great victories and heavy losses suffered by the German Fighter Force against the crushing superiority of the Allied Air Forces in the air and when the gigantic errors in decisions by the *Luftwaffe* High Command have been evaluated, one can only draw the conclusion that the German people were defended by a hard and courageous *Luftwaffe* Fighter Force."

Glossary

Abort: Turn back from an aerial mission before completion.

Acceptable Loss: Combat loss judged not to be high for results obtained. Within the limits of affordable cost.

Airacobra: Nickname for the Bell P-39 fighter airplane.

Attrition: The process of permanent loss of aircraft due to enemy action or other operational or defined cause.

Ausbildangsabteilung: Training Branch.

B-17: Four-engine bomber by Boeing. "The Flying Fortress."

B-24: Four-engine bomber by Consolidated. The "Liberator."

B-25: Two-engine bomber by North American. The "Mitchell."

B-26: Two-engine bomber by Martin. The "Marauder."

Bandit: Pilot slang for an enemy aircraft.

Big Week: 20-25 February 1944. A maximum effort by Allied bombers against Germany's aircraft industry.

Blitz, Blitzkrieg: Highly mobile form of warfare introduced by the German Army, featuring close cooperation between fast-moving armored forces and air power. Old-style army units could not cope with these new techniques, which led to rapid victories. Literally, "flash war"; generally, lightning war.

Blue Max: top German decoration of World War II, officially the *Pour le Merité.*

Condor Legion: A volunteer Air Force made up from the *Luftwaffe* to gain experience in Spain in supporting General Franco, 1936-1939. In Germany it was termed Legion Kondor.

Day Fighter: A fighter airplane designed for use when the target can be seen in daylight.

Dogfight: An aerial battle between opposing fighter aircraft.

ETO: European Theater of Operations.

External Store: Any fuel tank, bomber, rocket, etc., attached externally to the wings or fuselage of an airplane.

Fat Dog: *Luftwaffe* expression for large bombers loaded with bombs. Sometimes called "fat target"-a target of considerable value.

Fat One:

Feldwebel: Flight Sergeant.

Fliegerdivision: An Air Division.

Fliegerhorstkommandant: Airfield Commandant.

Fliegerkorps: Air Command Office (Operational).

Four-engine: A four-engine bomber. In World War II these were generally the British Halifax, Stirling, Lancaster, and Lincoln; American four-engines were the Boeing B-17 Fortress and Consolidated B-24 Liberator.

*Führer*hauptquartier: *Führer* Headquarters.

Fuerangsstab: Operations Staff.

Fw 190: The Focke-Wulf single-engine fighter plane.

General der Jagdflieger: General of the Fighter Pilots.

General der Kampfflieger: General of the Bomber Forces.

Generalstab: General Staff.

Geschwader: The largest mobile, homogeneous formation in the *Luftwaffe*. In the *Luftwaffe* a Fighter Wing (Jagd*geschwader*) consisted of three *Gruppen*.

Thus:

A Wing consisted of three *Gruppen* (Groups)

    A *Gruppen* consisted of three *Staffeln* (Squadrons)

    A *Staffel* consisted of three *Schwarmen*

Each *Schwarm* consisted of four aircraft, and was divided into two *Rotten*. The *Rotte* of two aircraft was the basic tactical element.

Geschwaderkommodore: The Wing Commander. Usually a Colonel or Lieutenant Colonel; sometimes a Major, very rarely, a Captain.

Gruppe: A Group. Usually consisted of three Squadrons. Largest (thirty-six aircraft) individual operational unit of the *Luftwaffe* fighter force.

Gruppenkommandeur: Group Commander. Usually a Major, sometimes a Captain.

Hauptquartier: Headquarters.

Head-on: A frontal attack.

Horrido!: The victory cry of the *Luftwaffe* fighter pilots. Also a greeting and parting word among friends and comrades of the *Luftwaffe*. It is actually the cry of the hunter when he sights the quarry. It was the typical German hunting cry.

Inspekteur der Nachtjaeger: Inspector of Night Fighters.

Inspekteur der Tagjaeger: Inspector of Day fighters.

Jabo: Abbreviation for fighter-bomber.

Jafü: Abbreviation of Jagdfuhrer, fighter Leader. Separate fighter commands in each Luftflotte. Originally assigned a policy-regulating and observing role, Fighter Leaders later controlled operations and handled considerable administration.

Jagdgeschwader: Fighter Wing. Usually consisted of three or four *Gruppen* of pilots and aircraft. From 108 to 144 aircraft made up the establishment of Wing. Some were larger. See under *Geschwader*.

Jagdstaffel: Fighter Squadron.

Kadetten Korps: Cadet Corps.

Karinhall: Göring's estate on the Shorfheide, about twenty-five miles north of Berlin.

Kette: Basic three-ship element used in early *Luftwaffe* fighter tactics, the counterpart of the RAF's three-ship "Vic" formation. Replaced in the *Luftwaffe* before World War II by the *Rotte and Schwarm* formations; returned with the Me 262.

Ketten*Führer*: Flight Commander.

Kommodore: Abbreviation of the *Geschwaderkommodore*. C.O. of a Wing.

Kriegsgliederung: Battle Order.

Lehrgeschwader: Training, tactical, and experimental Wing.

Leutnant: Lieutenant.

Lightning: The Lockheed P-38, a single-seat twin-boom fuselaged fighter aircraft.

Lufberry Circle: A formation in which two or more aircraft follow each other in flight circles in order to protect one another from enemy aircraft. Named for Major Raoul Lufbery, American ace who developed the tactic in World War I.

Luftflotten: Tactical and territorial air commands. Literally, Air Fleets.

Luftflottenkommando: Air Fleet HQ.

Luftgaue: Administrative and supply organizations of the *Luftwaffe*.

Luftwaffe: Air Force. The name of the German Air Force from 1935 through1945.

Bf 109: officially known as the Bf 109, Germany's most famous single-engine fighter. Originally designed by Bayerische Flugzeugwerke A.G. at Augsburg.

Me 262: The Messerschmitt twin-engined jet fighter.

NachtjagdGeschwader: Night Fighter Wing, abbreviated as NJG, followed by the number of the Wing, e.g., NJG 6.

Oberkommando der Luftwaffe: Referred to as OKL, the *Luftwaffe* High Command.

Oberkommando des Heeres: Referred to as OKH, the Army High Command.

Oberleutnant: First Lieutenant.

Oberst: Colonel.

Oberstleutnant: Lieutenant Colonel.

OKH: Army High Command.

OKW: High Command of the Armed Forces.

RAF: Royal Air Force.

RLM: *Reichluftfahrministerium,* the Air Ministry.

Rotte: A two-plane formation. Smallest tactical element in the *Luftwaffe* fighter force.

Rottenflieger: Wingman.

RottenFührer: Leader of a *Rotte*. Loosely, an element leader.

Schiessschule der Luftwaffe: *Luftwaffe* Gunnery School.

SchlachtGeschwader: Ground Attack Wing, or Close Support Wing.

Schwarm: Two-*Rotten* formation, four or five aircraft acting in a single flight. Three *Schwarme* flying together made up a *Staffel*, or Squadron.

SchwarmFührer: Leader of a *Schwarm.*

Sortie: A flight or sally of a single airplane, which penetrates into airspace where enemy contact may be expected. While a single plane or any number of aircraft may go out on a mission, each aircraft flying is actually making a sortie. One mission may involve any number of sorties.

Split-ess: A high-speed maneuver in which the airplane makes a half-roll onto its back and then dives groundward, leveling off going in the opposite at a much lower altitude.

Stabs-Schwarm: A head quarters flight of three to six aircraft, usually of the same type that make up the *Geschwader*. The Wing Commander and his Adjutant normally fly in the *Stabs-Schwarm*.

Staffel: A Squadron. Consisted of three *Schwarms*, made up from twelve to fifteen aircraft. Three or sometimes four *Staffeln* made up a *Gruppe*.

St. Horridus: The Savior Saint of the *Luftwaffe* fighter pilots and origin of the victory cry "Horrido!"

Thunderbolt: Popular name for the Republic P-47 fighter airplane.

Unteroffizier: A rank equivalent to an U.S. Army Sergeant or a USAF Airman First Class. This rank is above the German Obergefreiter (Senior Corporal) and below the rank of Unterfeldwebel (Staff Sgt.). Unteroffizier is the lowest non-commissioned officer rank, hence "Under Officer."

Verbandsführer: Unit commander.

Verteidigungszone West: Western Air Defense Zone.

Waffengeneral: Technical Service General.

Wilde Sau: Literally, Wild Boar, name of a German night fighter unit operating without radar aids in single-engine fighters.

Zerstörer: Literally, Destroyer. The name chosen for the long-range, twin-engine Bf 110 fighter (Bf 110). Destroyer Wing. Fighter Wings consisting of Bf 110s, expressed as ZG 26, ZG 1, etc.

Bibliography

Brickhill, Paul. *Reach for the Sky, Story of Douglas Bader:* Great Britain: Fontana Books, 1984.

Caldwell, Donald. *JG 26: Top Guns of the Luftwaffe:* New York, NY: Ivy Books-published by Ballantine Books, 1993.

Forrester, Larry. *Fly for Your Life, The Story of Robert Stanford Tuck:* Great Britain: published by Fredrick Muller, 1986.

Galland, Adolf. *The First and the Last*: New York, NY: Ballantine Books, Inc., 1957.

Johnson, Group Captain J.E. *Full Circle:* New York, NY: Ballantine books, 1964.

Johnson, Group Captain Johnnie. *Wing Leader*: Great Britain: Chatto & Windus, 1956.

Jullian, Marcel. *The Battle of Britain:* New York, NY: Fawcett Publications, 1968.

Killan, John. *The Luftwaffe A History*: Great Britain: Published by Fredrick Muller, Ltd., 1967.

Speer, Albert. *Inside the Third Reich.*

Index